A look at
BLACK HISTORY

in the
UK & WORLDWIDE

A Beginners Guide to
'Who You Are'

The Investigator

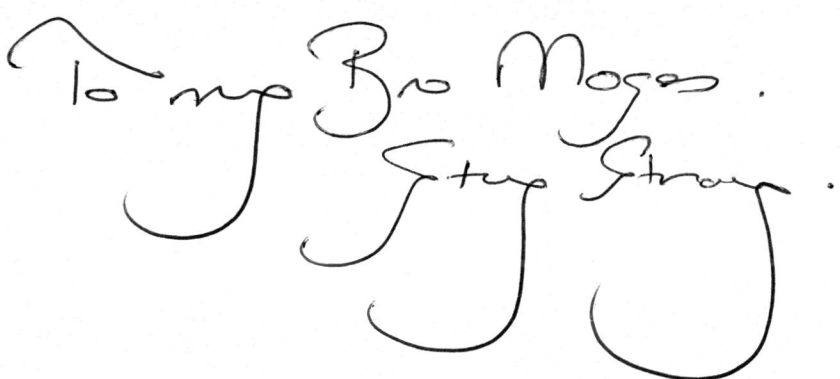

THE HIDDEN TRUTH

"FREE YOUR MIND"

by

Andrew Muhammad
A.K.A, 'The Investigator'

8/12/18

Free Your Mind
Copyright © 2004 Andrew Muhammad
a.k.a 'The Investigator'
First published 2004 Hakiki Publishing, London

2nd Edition - Reprint

TamaRe House Publishers
25 Brixton Station Road
London, SW9 8PB
United Kingdom
www.tamarehouse.co.uk

Printed in the United Kingdom
All rights reserved
ISBN: 978-1-906169-30-5

Cover picture of Brain
Copyright © 2004 Science Photo Library

WHO AM I?

Yes, who are you?
Don't tell me Negro - that's nothing.

Who were you before the Man named you Negro?
Where were you?
What did you have?
What was yours?
What language did you speak?
What was your name?

And why don't you know what your name was?
Where did it go?
Where did you lose it?
Who took it?
What tongue did you speak?
How did the man take your tongue?

Where is your history?
How did the man wipe out your history?
What did the man do to make you as dumb?
as you are right now?

Yes, the question is

WHO AM I?

(Malcolm X)

V

THE INVESTIGATOR

Dedication

This book is dedicated first and foremost to the one true and living Creative Force which has many names and attributes but without whom there would be no existence.

Free Your Mind is also dedicated to the Ancestors, as a token of thanks and praise and to say to all those who paved the way - your blood, sweat and tears were not in vain.

To my parents, Daphne and Melbourne, I give special thanks for the love and wisdom in my upbringing.

To my children Elijah, Sharifah, Malika-Zaynah and Kamil, I pray that you will dedicate your lives to the resurrection of your people and all oppressed people worldwide.

To Minister Michael Muhammad, you know this book would not be possible without your guidance and patience. I thank you from the bottom of my heart.

Peace.

Andrew Muhammad
A.K.A
'The Investigator'

Making **history** something to look **forward** to.

Andrew Muhammad is one of the United Kingdom's very few Black history and Culture specialists.

His lively lectures and courses are designed to bring history and culture to life, whereby the listener will fall in love with the rich culture and proud achievements of Black people worldwide.

He has developed his own brand of presentation called 'The Hidden Truth Breakdown', where the lectures are backed by passages from a range of sources. These include books that are considered very rare collectors' items but most are readily available in general bookstores and libraries. The sci-fi series, X files is correct by using the cliché 'The truth is out there'.

Hence the name Hidden Truth is given because the truth of our history and culture is in the very books we overlook or have been kept from us.

Andrew Muhammad has also designed what is widely known as the 'Hidden Truth Movie Breakdown'. This delivery is based on the Chinese proverb that a picture paints a thousand words.

The movie industry has perfected the art of using signs and symbols to convey many hidden truths to a very unsuspecting and susceptible audience. This type of communication was first invented in Kemet (Egypt) and was used in their mystery schools in the Nile civilisation.

Many household films and cartoons contain secrets that will amaze the viewers. It is the job of the 'Investigator' to reveal just what those secrets are. His delivery is suitable to all, regardless of age or attention span.

What makes the Hidden Truth lectures and Movie Breakdowns so unique is that they are so easy to follow and understand. The Investigator puts the fun back into learning.

He is available for lectures, seminars, courses, debates, interviews and mentoring and he provides talks on a wide range of topics covering:

World History; Kemet (Egypt), India, Africa, The Middle East, Europe, Australia, Britain, Central America and the Caribbean.

The Creative Arts; Films, Movies, Cartoons

History of Fashion

Science and Inventors

Secret Societies and Orders

Self Development, Improving Study techniques, How to improve memory, Community of Self and much more.

Further Info: www.theinvestigator.org.uk

Introduction

What you are about to read in this book may be unbelievable to some because it wasn't taught in the local state schooling system, announced by Trevor McDonald on the 10 o'clock news or reported in the Daily Snooze papers. Yet you will find it is the TRUTH.

"If there is anything you want to hide from a Black Man put it in a BOOK; that will be the last place he would look". This is a popular maxim used by the so-called 'rulers' of the world for over 400 years - sadly, it has been largely proven true. This generation must put an end to the above quote by reclaiming our stolen heritage.

Hiding the truth is a very serious thing to do. It causes harm and disappointment and causes one to be misled. The greatest and gravest hiding of truth is the truth that will make you mentally free. Jesus says in the New Testament, "You shall know the truth and the truth shall set you free".

Once you have acquired knowledge, it is a sin not to share it. You have a responsibility to pass it on. Once you have done this you have fulfilled your mission.

Contents

Chapter 1

Is it possible that the white race was first?   1
    Who is the original man?   1
    A man by his word   4

Chapter 2

Earth was our home and Africa was our throne   6
    Egypt   7
    India   14
    Ancient America   17
    Arabia   20
    China and Japan   24

Chapter 3

Hidden Truth   26
    Ancient Europe   26
    The true owners of Europe   27
    Venus – The original Queen of Europe   30
    Iberia – The land of the little giants   35
    Was Greek civilisation Black or White?   36

Chapter 4

The African Origins of the United Kingdom   41
    If you don't like it go back to where you come from   41
    The mysterious Red Man   43
    The land that time forgot   45
    Early Black tribes of Britain   47
    The Blackamoors of Britain   49
    A name is worth Moor than gold   52
    The last Black King of Britain   57
    The Black Vikings of Denmark   58

Chapter 5

Remnants of a long lost culture   63
    The original root's rockers   63
    The Black and White Minstrel Show   65
    Bring in the Clowns   67

Chapter 6

Who built Stonehenge?   70
    Other Stone Circles   77

Chapter 7

The very dark ages   80
    The Birth of the Roman Empire   80
    Rome gets an African Emperor   81
    Hells Angels Wreak Havoc in Europe   83

Chapter 8

Behold I will place you in a strange land for 400 years   85
    The Renaissance – The door, the way and the black light   85
    Biting the hand that feeds you   89
    1555-The worst crime in history   93
    The Arab slave trade   95
    The numbers game   97

Chapter 9

The forming of the Black Community in England   99
    A few good men   100
    The James Somerset Case   101
    The Black Loyalists   103
    The British Empire   105
    From Windrush to Winds of Change-
    Respect due to that First Generation   107

Conclusion   110

References   115

Chapter 1

Is it possible that the white race was first?

WHO IS THE ORIGINAL MAN?

The above question is a critical question to answer. Does it mean that whoever is first is necessarily superior to those who came after? The answer is, emphatically, NO.

Yet religious experts and scientist agree that from one blood came all human beings and like any intelligent child we should want to know whom our parents were, where they lived and what they looked like.

When anthropologists (people who study man's origin) try to find mans beginnings they never stay too long in Europe, they always take their studies to the Eastern lands of Africa and Asia.

The most famous anthropologists were the British Leakey family - husband wife and son. They made important discoveries in Eastern Africa concerning man's origin.

In 1959 Mary Leakey found a human skull nearly 2 million years old in Northern Tanzania.

She named the fossil remains *Zinjanthropus*, ('zinj' meaning black and 'antropus' meaning man) - in other words the black man. Yet it was agreed by later scientists to rename it *Australopithecus boisei* (the southern ape man).[1] This was a racist attempt to conceal the true identity of the original man.

The Leakey family kept on digging and found earlier fossils belonging to the Black Nation going back over 14 million years and each new discovery showed that the fossil had a mother and a father. No scientist to date has been able to trace the origin of the Black man.

Both science and religion agree that Man has a common origin. They also agree by inference that man originated in the tropics - in an environment where food and shelter were most easily accessible.[2] The Garden of Eden has been placed by scholars in what is now mislabelled the Middle East and, by others, in East Africa.[3]

The Holy Qur'an (the Holy book of the Muslims) shines light on creation of the first man. The book states in the 15th Chapter that,
"Surely Man was made from Black mud fashioned into shape,"

The Bible teaches that from one blood came all.

The modern father of genetic science the Austrian botanist and monk, Gregor J. Mendel formulated the basic laws of heredity. These laws are known as Mendel Laws.[4] He states dark eyes, hair and skin are dominant and blue eyes, and pale skin and blonde hair are recessive. His studies proved that you can get the recessive from the dominant but you cannot get the dominant from the recessive.

In simpler terms you can get pale skin from dark skin but not dark skin from pale skin. Two blue/black people in the darkest parts of African can produce a jet-black baby or a person with pale skin, blonde hair and blue eyes called today albinos (from Latin 'albus' meaning white).
The German philosopher Arthur Schopenhaur said,

> **"There is no such thing as a white race, but every white man is a faded out or bleached Black man".[5]**

Ancient Greek writers such as Herodotus and Diodorus Siculus both record that the Ethiopians were the first men on Earth.[6]

A MAN BY HIS WORD

Wise people study words because contrary to widespread belief, words do not just float down from the sky. Many words convey deep hidden truths. The science of etymology (the origin and meaning of words) tells us that the first human was of colour.

Let's look at a few words in the <u>Collins English Dictionary</u> used to describe original people:

Aborigine: A member of a dark skinned hunting and gathering people: a Black. 'Ab' means father or from, 'Origine' means the beginning, so Aborigine = The father of beginning.

Native: A member of indigenous peoples of a country or area especially a NON White. From the Latin *nativus* meaning natural. So Native = The natural beings of earth

Human: The Earth's man. From humus
the dark organic material in soil
which is essential to the fertility of
the earth. The dark man made
from the soil of the earth.

Dr Charles Finch informs us that the ancient Egyptian word for the African lands south of Egypt was *Khenti - Khentiu* denoting the Sudanic peoples who lived there. This word is also their word for 'first', 'foremost', 'beginning', 'origin' and 'chief'.[7]

Chapter 2

Earth was our home and Africa was our throne

We need a global view of Black people. I truly agree with our great sister historian, Drusilla Dunjee Houston (1876-1941) that there seems to be a worldwide conspiracy to conceal the facts that books like this unfold. Because of this suppression of truth, world crimes have been easily made possible against Black people.[8]

The understanding given to us from the western scholars which is then backed up by Hollywood and the powerful media machinery, is that prior to the European Greek civilisation, man was basically savage and living in caves or mud huts.

They teach us that Black people never existed on the world scene until we were discovered in the jungles of Africa living like apes. (Reflect on films like Tarzan). This cannot be further from the truth.

EGYPT

The killing fields have done an excellent job on our minds with regards to Egypt. I was in college before I even realised that Egypt was in AFRICA and not this so-called mystical Middle East. (Man I was DUMB!).

The Egyptians of today are not the same as the ancient Egyptians of 5000 years ago, just as American's today are not the same as the Native Americans of 500 years ago. Assyrians, Syrians, Persians and Europeans populate Egypt today. Their migration into this land has been in process for over 2000 years. They have painted Egypt as a white or pale skinned civilisation.

According to the World Book Encyclopaedia under the heading 'Ancient Egypt' it states the BLACK-haired, DARK-skinned ancient Egyptians were short and slender. They belonged to the EUROPEAN geographical race.

Wait a minute! Can you believe these racists so-called academics! Just think dear reader; I have been travelling to Egypt for the last nine years at the time of the writing of this book.

Egypt is in North East Africa. It has a clear dry climate, the atmosphere has a brilliance which is intolerable, the torrid sun is unrelieved by any shade and rain rarely falls. This environment only suits a people who have a body natural to the sun and soaked in melanin (the black or brown pigmentation in the skin, eyes and hair).

It is well known that pale skinned people have a major problem living in the sun because it gives them cancer and many other ailments. Also would it not be more probable that since Egypt is in Africa that Africans got there before Europeans and built civilisation?

The wise know the truth. In the book Arab and Israel for Beginners, Ron David, (who incidentally is a Caucasian American) admits that Western historians have a problem with Egypt for two main reasons: Egypt is the granddaddy of Western civilisation and is based in Africa. Which then leads to the second problem, they like to think that,

"The Egyptians were white guys with rust on their faces. However the fact is that they were overwhelmingly Black Africans".

This fact, Ron David goes on, is obvious in many portraits and steles. This was missed by most archaeologists because, self-referring racists that they were, they did not realise that they were looking at Black Africans. They thought that they were looking at deformed white people.

There was no such place called Egypt in ancient times. The people referred to their land as 'Kemet' or 'Chemmet' - The Black Land, and themselves as 'Kemmiu' - The Blacks.

Anthony T. Browder in his superb book Nile Valley Contributions to Civilization writes that the word 'Kemiu' was also used to describe the vast population that inhabited the Nile. In ancient times there was not a physical distinction made between the people in the land now called Egypt, and the Sudan.

Herodotus the 'Greek' father of History is studied at Oxford, Cambridge and Yale. He is the major authority on Egypt for the Western world.

He travelled to Egypt 2500 years ago and stated that gods on earth inhabited Egypt. He wrote that among these male and female gods was one supremely wise, known as the Supreme Being.

Herodotus a man who walked and talked with the ancient Egyptians described them as

9

BLACK! and compares them to the ETHIOPIANS[9].

He says, further, that these Ethiopians were wise men occupying the Upper Nile, "men of long life, whose manners and customs pertain to the Golden Age, those virtuous mortals whose feast and banquets are honoured by Jupiter himself".

In those early ages Egypt was under Ethiopian domination. In proof of this fact the Encyclopaedia of Biblical Literature says that Isaiah often mentions Ethiopia and Egypt in close political relations.

In fact the name of Ethiopia chiefly stood as the name of the national and royal family of Egypt.

Experts are still baffled by the technology used by the ancient Blacks of Kemet. Their advanced knowledge of the sciences where known as ALCHEMY, (a compound word 'al' = the, and 'chemy' = black).

Today alchemy is called black magic. From alchemy (the Blacks magic) we have the modern words 'CHEMist', 'CHEMistry' and 'CHEMicals'. The pictures on the Egyptian monuments reveal that Africans were the builders.

These gods of the Old World left testimonies that will live forever.

The Great Pyramid is the largest, oldest and the last remaining of the Seven 'Wonders of the World.' It stands at 481 feet with 201 stair-stepped tiers. It is made of approximately two and a half million blocks of stone weighing an average of two and a half tons each. In the Kings Chamber there are several blocks that weigh in excess of 70 tons, the equivalent of a railroad locomotive.

Listen, there is more stone in this one structure than in all the cathedrals, churches and chapels in England since the coming of Christ. Here, there is enough stone to build 30 Empire State buildings.

If the stones were cut into one-foot blocks and laid end to end, they would stretch two thirds of the distance around the earth at the equator.

The cement used to bind these stones in place is 1/50 of an inch, the thickness of two sheets of paper, and is nearly invisible when compared to the one-half inch of mortar used in the so-called modern brick industry today.

The Pyramids base covers 13.11 square acres. The base is perfectly level to within one-half inch. It is the most perfectly aligned building to true north.[10]

With just these few facts, (and believe me there are many more), if you were to give the most modern construction engineer the task to build such a structure, he would probably say, "Impossible!" To make matters worse, the builders - Chemites (Blacks) - left not one piece of evidence to say how or when they built it.

They only left evidence as to WHO built it and it was not little green men! In 1996 there was a discovery of a secret shaft in the Queens Chamber inside the Great Pyramid by Rudulf Gantenbrink. (At the end of this shaft was a sealed door.

On 20th October 1996, at 9.30am Cairo time, a team had managed to get a robot borne fibre - optic probe through a flaw in the door.

This revealed a small chamber. Inside, was a statute of a seated BLACK MALE, feet and knees crossed, holding on to an ankh (key of life). This BLACK MALE was gazing out of the shaft looking towards Sirius (a star linked to many African tribes and their mythologies).

Why was this discovery not on every news report? Yet David Beckham (the footballer) can decide to change his hairstyle and the tribes in the deepest regions of the Amazon would know about it. Smile ☺

The Greek writer Herodotus says that with all the magnanimity and excellence of the Great Pyramid he saw another structure that surpassed it. He said this building was BEYOND his POWER to even describe.

This monument cost MORE in labour and money than ALL the walls and public works of the Greeks put TOGETHER, (we have all heard how great the Greeks were).[11]

This building was simply one of the homes of the Nubian Pharaoh Amenhemet III. Many of us would dream to live in a 10-bedroom house; we would need to stretch our minds to imagine a 100-room house. Yet over 4000 years ago this Black man was living large!

He built a split-level palace with over 3000 rooms, 12 covered courtyards - 6 facing north and 6 facing south. Herodotus, who wrote from an eyewitness account further, goes on to say,

"The baffling and intricate passages from room to room and from court to court were an endless wonder".

13

The walls were covered with carved figures and each court was exquisitely built of white marble and surrounded by a colonnade. In the corner of this building stood a 240ft pyramid. The Greeks called this monument the Labyrinth because of its complexity.[12] We need to recreate Kemet all over again and end this lie that we were found simply with bones in our noses singing the praises of the Great Tarzan

INDIA

Historic India is not a country. It is a culture, one of the oldest and most consistent on Earth. Some scholars believe this culture to be as old as Egypt. The word India derives from Indus, the sacred river of India. According to the esteemed scholar Drusilla Houston, the very word Indus means Black and it was used to designate the home of the Asiatic Ethiopians. She says even the name Hindu is Ethiopian at root.[13]

The Greek writer Philostratus in Vit. Apollon (Lib II) says:
"The Indi are the wisest of mankind. The Ethiopians are a colony of them and they inherit the wisdom of their fathers".

The separation of India from their parent African stock happened long before the rise of the European Aryan Race that inhabited India today.

Marco Polo described the inhabitants of India as black and adorned with massive gold bracelets and strings of rare and precious gems. They had temples and priests.

One of Walt Disney's most famous productions **Jungle Book** gives hints to these original people.

When the monkeys in the Jungles of India abducted Moglee he was taken to the ruling ape, King Louie, (the trumpeter Louis Armstrong supplied the voiceover). These monkeys were given obvious black voices and sounded like brothers from the ghetto.

In the film the monkeys' territory was called the Ancient Ruins. In other words they ruled long ago and their empire is now destroyed.

Walt Disney (a well known racist who once stated that he would never employ a Black in his studio) was admitting that the Black Nation were the true owners of that land but wanted to give the impression that they were uncivilised and behaved like apes and monkeys.

Yet we have evidence still standing today that Europe was not able to match their achievements till thousands of years later.

The religion of Buddha of India is well known to be very ancient. In ancient temples scattered throughout India, where his worship is still continued, he is found to be jet black, with the flat face, thick lips, and curly hair of the Black Man. Several statues of the most ancient Buddha's can be seen today in the museum of the East-India Company.[14]

Another ancient god of India is Krishna. The word Krishna literally means he with the Black face. Krishna is constantly called Heri-Krishna: this is the black. Krishna represented the masses of the aboriginal people of Asia who were fighting the invading Aryans over the control of the land.[15]

Mr Maurice, the famed mathematician, says in Volume 1 of Indian Antiquities, that the figures in the caves in India and in the temples in Egypt are absolutely the same.[16]

The scholar Sir W Jones says that the connection between Africa and India is very intimate. He studied many of the monuments of antiquity in India and found that the letters on many of the monuments appeared partly Indian and partly Ethiopian. The mountaineers of Bengal and Bahar can hardly be distinguished in some of their features (particularly the nose and lips) from modern Ethiopians.

The Honourable Elijah Muhammad (Spiritual Leader of the Nation of Islam) teaches that the Indians and Africans are but one universal Black nation. According to Strabo (Greek geographer and historian 63 B.C) the Hindus (Indians) differed in nothing from the Africans but in the straightness and smoothness of their hair, while that of the African was crisp or woolly.[17]

ANCIENT AMERICA

According to the Ancient America Encyclopaedia, Jonathan Norton Leonard in his book The Great Ages of Man, A History of the Worlds Cultures states:

"Until very recently no one knew when or where the first civilisation of Middle America got started. The whole region is cluttered with enigmatic ruins, enormous stone temples, gigantic pyramids and carvings standing mysteriously alone. Few of these relics are identified even by legend. Most were known to the Indians of historic times only as the place where the gods once came to earth".

He goes on further to say that with modern technology archaeologists (specialists who study man's past by the material remains of his culture) have made outstanding discoveries.

"In many parts of Mexico they found strange and characteristic figures in stone, pottery or jade. Most of them had thick Negroid (African) lips and flat noses". Indeed these gods were no other than the Original Black Man. Sculptures of these kinds were found plentiful in the Mexican States of Tabasco and Veracruz on the Gulf Coast. These people are today called the Olmecs.

The Original nation was there so long ago that the period is considered prehistory. In the old poems of Nahuatl (the language of the Aztecs) it tells of a land on the eastern sea that was settled so long ago that 'no one can remember.' "

Ivan Van Sertima records that in 1938 Dr Mathew W Stirling of the Smithsonian Institution discovered a stone of a Black Man's head, six and a half feet tall and weighing ten tons, near the village of Tres Zapotes. Nearby they found pyramids of clay over 110 feet high.[18]

Many more stone heads were found on the Island of La Venta. They weighed in excess of 45 tons yet no stone is found on this island.

No one really knows how they transported these enormous heads such far distances over land and water. These huge Afrikanoid images were also found on Easter Island and other islands of the Pacific Ocean.

One of the first offshoot centres set up by the Olmecs was Monte Alban, near the Mexico City of Oaxaca. This impressive group of stone pyramids and other ceremonial buildings stand on a mountain spur that looms high above three fertile valleys.

The structures now visible were built long after the Olmec times, but archaeologists tunnelled into them and found earlier buildings, some of which contained large flat stones with Olmec-like figures carved in bas-relief. The stones had been used merely as construction material and must have belonged to a still-older structure that was torn down.

The bas-reliefs are called danzantes or the dancers. They depicted naked men in strange poses. The carvings show very thick lips and flat noses of Africans. The carvers are said to be the Zapotes Indians who still live in that area.

These Indians were strongly influenced by their ancestors, the Olmecs. The oldest writings found in Ancient America belong to the Olmecs. There are many hieroglyphs that have still not been satisfactorily interpreted by today's scientists.

ARABIA

According to the <u>World Book Encyclopaedia</u>, two of the world's first great civilisations - Ancient Egypt and Babylon - and the three major religions, Islam, Christianity and Judaism, were born in the so-called Middle East.

Have you ever thought to yourself where or what is the Middle East? This was a term created recently to hide the reality that the Middle East is Northern Africa - the cradle of civilisation. In terms of its general features, Arabia resembles the African Sahara of which it is a continuation. The history of Arabia needs to be re-written.

Ordinary encyclopaedias and historical books give but little light on the aboriginal life and people of that area. Arabia was one of the original seats of Ethiopian culture. Indeed, the great spiritual leader of the Lost but now Found Members of the Nation of Islam in the West - The Honourable Elijah Muhammad, teaches that Arabia was the centre of learning for the Ancient Black Nation of Asia.

The Asiatic (Black) nation has 24 supremely wise scientists that would meet every 25,000 years in the Holy City of Mecca to write the world's history.[19]

Archaeologists are still digging in that part of the world looking for what they call the hall of records. This chamber is meant to hold the writings of these scientists.

Why was Mecca chosen? The word Mecca actually means centre. Mecca was the centre or the hub of our civilisation. There are pictures and images in Egypt that showed that in very ancient times the Egyptians conducted pilgrimages to Mecca long before there was a man called Muhammad and a religion called Islam.

In the early traditions and records of Greece, Arabia is described as Ethiopia. In Richard Stoneman's Encyclopaedia of Myth and Legend -

<u>Greek Mythology</u>, under the word Arab it says, "an evil spirit in the form of Black Man". Further, Ancient Greek writers such as Strabo, Pliny, Diodorus and Ptolemy write about the high cultured civilisation of Southern Arabia.

Two distinct people, an earlier Cushite (Ethiopian) and a much later so-called Semitic Arabian, originally settled there. The Cushites are the aboriginal Arabians and dwelt there long before there was an Abraham. These aboriginal Arabians were the Adites, Thamudites and the Anu.

The purest and oldest blood of Arabia belongs to these Nubians (Blacks). They left stupendous ruins to be found in every part of that country. At the time that Ethiopians began to show power as Pharaohs of Egypt, about 3000 BC, the western part of Arabia was divided into two powerful kingdoms.

In those days the princes belonged to the descendants of the Ethiopians who ruled from Yemen (Southern Arabia) for thousands of years.[20]

The 105th chapter of the Holy Qur'an is called The Elephant, after the Abyssinian (Ethiopian) King Abrahah who ruled Yeman. According to

Islamic historians he tried to invade Mecca in 570 AD using his army of elephants[21].

In the book Muhammad the Prophet, Maulana Muhammad Ali states that Yemen is the most fertile part of Arabia and thus the most civilised. Yemen was the centre of trade in minerals, precious stones and spices for which the country is now famous.

He says that Ad, Thamud, Tasm and Jadis are the most ancient tribes. These tribes are known as Baidah (ancient Arabs) or Aribah (pure Arabs).

The present day Arabians we see there today are referred to as Musta 'ribah (naturalised Arabs).

Modern historians tell of the early Arabian conquests of Babylon but do not explain that these Arabs were the pure blooded African Arabians. The Encyclopaedia Britannica in its article on Arabia says:

"The institutions of Yemen bear a close resemblance to African types of the Nile Valley. This land was under the rule of the Southern race."

These kings ruled Arabia and Central Asia to the boundaries of China. The Nubians were their mothers and their rulers were her rulers.

CHINA AND JAPAN

Have you ever taken a good look at a Chinese or Japanese person? Apart from the skin colour you are looking at African people in their physical features, the breadth of face, high cheekbones and flat nose. The first people of China were the Blacks of antiquity. There are unmixed Black people with no apparent connection to Africa still living in Southern China today.

According to the French anthropologist H. Imbert who lived in the Far East, he says:

"The Black people at some time occupied all of South India, Indo China and China. In the South of Indo-China are the Semangs, Malays and the Sakais, all of which are members of the Black family. Skulls of these Blacks have been found in the island of Formosa and Liu-Kiu south of Japan." [22]

In 1933 the US Department of Agriculture discovered an unmixed "Negro" type in China -

the Nakhis, numbering 200,000 – who, it said, had preserved their culture for over 2000 years.

Professor Munro, one of the foremost students of Japanese life and culture says:

"The Japanese are a mixture of several distinct stocks, African and Mongolian...." [23]

We should not be surprised at the Black origin of the Japanese. Just take a look at the islands surrounding Japan, her neighbours are mainly Black too - the Philippines and Pacific islands.

In the book <u>Signs and Symbols of Primordial Man</u> it states that the Ainu are the oldest known people in Japan. They are of the same original race and type as the Australian Aborigines and their beliefs and rituals correspond with those of the ancient Egyptians. Their skulls and the shape of their heads are the same as the Australians and Ethiopians. [24]

Chapter 3

Hidden Truth

ANCIENT EUROPE

Black people may find it hard to believe that Europe was not always cold, frosty, wet, dull and frigid. Coal and oil deposits are a sign that the region was once tropical.

The environment of Europe was once similar to the Caribbean and Mother Africa. The warrior scholar Reverend Ishakamusa Barashango (author of Afrikan people and European Holidays: A Mental Genocide), writes that the whole earth was an Eden-like paradise.

If we look at Planet Asia (the original name for Earth), the landmasses that we call continents were once connected - joined together. There was universal unity on the Earth.

Planet Asia was covered in a warm beautiful ambience. All over the world even as far as Greenland and the Arctic Circle, fossils of elephants, hippopotami, rhinoceroses, camels, lions and other tropical animals have been discovered.

Reverend Barashango reminds us that during that time Earth is described as having a thriving luxuriant tropical paradise with palm trees, magnolias, sequoias and a myriad of other flourishing trees and plants.[25]

THE TRUE OWNERS OF EUROPE

The English scholar Godfrey Higgins says in his book <u>Anacalypsis</u> that the role of the Black man always featured in his research concerning the origin of man and of God, regardless of where he travelled and where he studied. There is no serious scientist, archaeologist or historian that will not admit that the Black Man of Africa is the first man of West Asia (Europe).

J.A Rogers says recent discoveries seems to indicate that the Black element proceeded the white and yellow everywhere..."the original colour of primitive man was black.... these earliest known human beings - of whom we have abundant evidence from their skeletons and their art form on all the continents - might have lived anywhere from 600,000 to 8,000 BC".[26]

The Black Man's history goes so far back in antiquity that dates become just a reference for convenience.

The supremely wise scientist of the Black Nation **Master Fard Muhammad** (Founder of the Nation of Islam) came from the mystical lands of the East and taught that the Black Man's history extends way back to over 76 trillion years. In all this time the Nubian Nation inhabited the whole Earth.[27]

During many of my lectures, brothers and sisters ask "How do you know all of this?" However they should be asking themselves why do THEY NOT KNOW ALL OF THIS? Why was this NOT taught in our schools when we were studying European History?

More recently, modern scholars have evidence that after the ice age of Europe another wave of Black Men spread their culture to all corners of the world including Southern and Western Europe in around 12,000 BC.

This mighty Black Man of Europe described by Dr Chiekh Anta Diop as 'tall with an extremely high skull', is designated Grimaldi by contemporary European archaeologists and anthropologists. This is because of the numerous remains and artefacts first found in modern times in a cave at Grimaldi in Italy.

According to the <u>Collins English Dictionary</u>, Grimaldi is defined as 'a type of man having a Negroid appearance'.

I believe it must have been so hard for them to admit that. What does a man having a Negroid appearance look like that is, himself, not a so-called Negroid (Black) man? Would it not be easier, and more to the point to define the Grimaldi as an African or Black man?

You see, many Black youth would never dream of looking up the word Grimaldi and if they did they must not be able to see and recognise the simple truth that they were rulers and originators of what we call Europe.

Legrand H Clegg II of Compton Community College, in 1969, wrote that the earliest man to occupy Europe was a prehistoric people called the Grimaldi. In support of his claim he cites skeletal and sculptural remains of these early Blacks that have been discovered in Europe over the past century, and presents proof of their African origins.[28]

In the book <u>Fossil Men</u>, Marcellin Bould and Henri Vallois, two of the world's foremost authorities on the prehistoric race known as Grimaldi, agree they are certainly Black and African.[29]

When the Nubian/Grimaldi first conquered Europe, he wielded his awesome fiery torch and he bore the emblem of the dragon.[30] This Nubian/Grimaldi brother must be studied and investigated more by our own scholars. Brothers and Sisters reading this book, I implore you: Never allow our past civilisations to be forgotten and lost. It may well be that the Creator placed us in Europe to resurrect our people's lost memories and contributions.

VENUS -THE ORIGINAL QUEEN OF EUROPE

The most famous early image of a human is a woman. She is called *Venus of Willendorf.* Now by the name we would never have known that this was one of our beautiful Black sisters in early Europe.[31] Found in 1908 by the archaeologist Josef Szombathy, in a heap of clay and silt deposited by the wind near the town of Willendorf in Austria, this image of 'Venus' is now in the Naturhistorisches Museum, Vienna.

The Venus of Willendorf is the most ancient human form in sculpture that we know. The statuette was carved from a particular type of limestone not found in the region and so must have been brought to the area from another location.

It may well be the case that the carving, which was presumably done with flint tools, was not done locally. A study published in 1990 of the nine superimposed archaeological layers comprising the Willendorf deposit indicates a date for the Venus of Willendorf of around 24,000-22,000 BCE.[32]

As the earliest known representation, she became the 'first woman', acquiring an Eve identity that focused suitably on the fascinating reality of the female body. She stands as a sexually charged embodiment of fertility; the woman from which all women descend.

There are paintings showing Nubian/Grimaldi artists holding the Venus of Willendorf. According to the *World Book Encyclopaedia* the Venus of Willendorf may have represented the Mother Goddess, who gave life to man and his food.

The most striking aspect of this sculpture is the shape of this female goddess. It tells us so much about her racial identity. The African Bushwomen-Hottentots is also noted for the same peculiar pear shape, huge breasts and large buttocks.[33]

At the time of its discovery, the statuette showed traces of red ochre pigment, which has been thought to symbolize the menstrual blood of women as a life-giving agent, as is the case in later traditions.

Current anthropology also provides examples of the custom among pregnant women of the Igbo of eastern Nigeria of carrying with them a red-painted wooden doll in a little bag, and of the use made of magic dolls by Zuni women in order to become pregnant or following a miscarriage.

There is also ample evidence from the historical period that the people of Kemet (Egypt) used red ochre to paint pharaohs on their temples. This red colouring represented the eternal life force of blood.[34]

This raises the possibility that the red ochre on the Venus served as a blood substitute and that the figurine may have served some purpose in connection with female menstruation. If this were the case it would increase the possibility that it was carved not by a man, but by a woman.

A characteristic of all Venus figurines showed by the Willendorf statuette is the lack of a face. Some argue that the face is a key feature in human identity, however the carver did not want us to concentrate on an individual person.

The carver felt that she is to be regarded as a symbol of all original women. It is her physical and spiritual body, and what it represents, that is important. From the front, the place where her face should be seems to be largely concealed by what are generally described as rows of African plaited hair wrapped around her head.[35]

Close examination, however, reveals that the rows are not one continuous spiral but are, in fact, comprised of seven horizontal bands that encircle the head, with two more half-bands below at the back of her neck. The top-most circle has the form of a rosette. The bands vary in width from front to back to sides, and also vary in size from each other.

Cut across the groove separating each band at regular, closely-spaced intervals is a series of more or less lozenge-shaped deep vertical notches, some wide, others narrow, that extend equally into the band above and into the band below. These notches alternate between bands to produce the effect of braided or plaited hair. That it is African braided hair seems clear.

When seen in profile, the impression is that the figure is looking down with her chin sunk to her chest, and her hair more resembles natural hair; longer at the back, and falling and gathering in the manner that human hair might on her upper back.

Some find it significant that the number of full circles of plaits is seven. Indeed, many thousands of years later seven was regarded as a magic number.

Sister Tynetta Muhammad (a world renowned Islamic scholar) teaches that the number seven is the number of Black people. It is result of the addition of the numbers 3 & 4 and denotes our hidden history in Egypt: The base of the each pyramid has four sides and supports the three-sided triangle above.

Sister Tynetta Muhammad also points to chapter 34 in the Holy Qur'an, which tells the history of the Tribe of Shabazz (an ancient name for the Black nation) through the story of the Queen of Sheba.[36]

Such elaborate treatment of hair is extremely rare in primitive figurines, and the considerable attention paid to it by the sculptor must mean it had some significance. In later cultures, hair has been considered a source of strength, and as the seat of the soul.

IBERIA – THE LAND OF THE LITTLE GIANTS

Reverend Barashango teaches that the Nubian/Grimaldi Man in Europe was succeeded by his shorter (in physical but not mental stature) brother, the *Twa*. The Twa is commonly referred to in scientific circles as the *Negrito* (a member of any of the dwarfish black peoples of South East Asia and Melanesia).[37]

These little Black Men were dubbed by later Greek historians as Iberians, so named after the Ebro River in Spain the centre of their cultural activities in Europe. These Black Iberians are the first known inhabitants of Spain and Portugal after the departure of the Nubian-Grimaldi.[38]

They are described as being short, swarthy, woolly-haired and robust. Their women had large posteriors (bottoms).[39]

According to the World Book Encyclopaedia, the name Iberia is the ancient name of the area occupied by Spain and Portugal today. It also states that the Iberians were one of the oldest

35

people of Europe. They came from Africa during prehistoric times, had swarthy skins and were short.

The Basques who now live in Northern Spain are thought to be their descendants. Their language still contains many Iberian words. Many other people living in Spain, Italy and Portugal are descended from Iberians.

WAS GREEK CIVILISATION BLACK OR WHITE?

The *Greeks* were the first civilised Europeans. Greece is a small country in Europe where the first European civilisation started more than 2000 years ago. Historians regard the Greeks as the founders of Western civilisation. However, we need to go beyond the 2000 years that are commonly quoted to find out who really was responsible for this very advanced society.

The story of Greece must begin in Crete (an island in the Aegean Sea, off the coast of mainland Greece). Cheikh Anta Diop states that throughout the entire Aegean area, the Black preceded the Indo-European. Originally all of the population of the Mediterranean were Black or Brown skinned people.

There is so much data available that links the Cretans (people of Crete) to the motherland of Africa. Evidence shows that Egyptians and Phoenicians held political and economic control and influence over that region for thousands of years.[40]

In Everyman's Encyclopaedia it states that these Cretans traded frequently with Africans in Kemet (Egypt) from the dawn of history. Kemet as discussed earlier was under the control of Nubians (Africans).

The encyclopaedia also states that in ancient Crete one of the most striking finds of this period was the discovery of their hieroglyphics, a special system of writing in which geometrical symbols represented syllables.

The Greeks later adapted this system to their own language. There was evidently a strong bond between the Nubians of Egypt and the Nubians of Crete.

Not only did these Cretans trade with their soul brothers of Africa but also they believed in the same gods.

In the book, The Civilisation of Greece in the Bronze Age, the author H.R.Hall refers to the fact that the Egyptian and the Cretan religion was linked and had many similarities.

Dr. John G. Jackson states that these Cretans were natives of *Alkebulan* (Africa). They were a branch of the western Ethiopian family. The cultural dominance of the Black Cretans is referred to today as the *Minoan civilisation*, after their King Minos.

These Black Cretans were truly great builders. They were skilled painters, master craftsmen, fine architects and adventurous sailors and traders. They built richly decorated palaces surrounded by massive walls. This whole island was literally littered with magnificent palaces, luxurious homes, well-constructed ports and paved streets.[41]

Try to picture the following: The king's palace was five stories high and covered over six acres. There was a paved central court, voluptuous halls and antechambers connected by beautifully decorated passages, well built and arranged.

There were wide stairways leading to spacious bathrooms with the most modern system of drainage, terracotta pipes and fresco paintings. These palaces were architectural masterpieces.[42]

The Cretans also developed a decimal numerical system of mathematics. According to later Greek writers there were over one hundred cities on Crete.

Crete's civilisation spread far and wide - evidence of their culture has been found as far away as Spain, Sardinia, Venice, Cyprus and Palestine.[43]

Between 1900 BC and 1450 BC a semi-barbarous tribe from the North laid this splendid culture to ruins. They invaded the Cretans and destroyed all their towns and palaces. Minoan culture declined and many of the skills the people developed simply disappeared. These invaders, according to historians, were the people we call Greeks.

According to the World Book Encyclopaedia these Greeks occupied Crete and copied Minoan architecture, pottery and customs. Soon the Greeks became very rich, and the most powerful people in the whole region. These invading Greeks became the first civilised white folks.

All we have left of the Minoan high cultured civilisation are stories and fables - myths - left by the Greeks, about a time when that whole area was inhabited by gods and goddesses who possessed knowledge of magic and had great powers.

Chapter 4

The African origins of the United Kingdom

"IF YOU DON'T LIKE IT GO BACK TO WHERE YOU CAME FROM!"

It makes me laugh when I watch the news and see how European Australians talk about being tough on immigration and not allowing any more refugees to 'swamp their country'. They seem to have forgotten that Australia was the home of the Black Aborigines and it was European riffraff from prisons, exiled there only a few hundred years ago, who have done the 'swamping'. It was the beneficence of the Aborigines that allowed them to 'immigrate' there and start a new life.

Likewise, would it not be funny if we could prove that Britain was the Black Man's land from the very beginning and we relaxed our immigration laws and allowed 'others' to live here, and now we are swamped by pale skinned immigrants? Well let's have a closer look, because historically that is exactly what happened.

It is a well-known biological fact that our colour is not only skin deep. One of the ways to determine the race of an individual is by the shape of the skull. The Black Man's skull is generally described by scientist as dolichocephalic (long skulls).[44]

In 1865 Mr Samuel Laing discovered a quantity of human remains near Kiess in the county of Caithness. Mr Samuel Laing wrote that these aboriginal Britons must have closely resembled the Australian Aborigines or Tasmanian.[45]

These remains were sent to Professor Huxley. In 1881 Professor Huxley in his pamphlet <u>The Early history of Scotland</u> says that the first inhabitants of Britain had skulls of the Black Man or Australian Aborigine.

The skulls found in chamber mounds in Great Britain are said by Dr Daniel Wilson to represent those of the earliest race in Britain. All of these skulls were generally long and narrow shaped (dolichocephalic) and proved to scientists that, without a shadow of a doubt, they belonged to

Black people. Mr Carter Blake, a competent judge, describes a skull from a cist (a box shaped burial chamber made from stone slabs), in Uist Island off Scotland, as being that of a Tasmanian.[46]

The Iberians inhabited the whole of present-day Spain, Portugal and Italy. While these Iberians were developing their civilisation in Europe we had the Black Nation of Buddha's in India spreading their eastern philosophy. Both of these nations were linked to their mother nation of Kemet (Egypt) via the mystery school system, which had headquarters in present day Luxor along the river Nile.

Members of the Australian Aborigines, Iberians, Indians and Egyptians travelled to many corners of unexplored lands. Indeed they came to the shores of the United Kingdom and were its first settlers.

THE MYSTERIOUS RED MAN

In 1823, Dr. Buckland discovered an ancient 'red coloured' body buried with rites in a Welsh cave. This discovery became known as the 'Red Man of Paviland'. In 1922, David A. Mackenzie wrote a book called <u>Ancient Man in Britain</u>. With reference to the 'Red Man of Paviland' he states that this find 'emphasises the Continental and North African influences that reached Britain'.

When found, the corpse was stained superficially with a dark brick-red colour, composed of red oxide of iron, which also stained the earth all around the body. The entire person must have been smothered with this red substance.

Mr Mackenzie wrote that this early man of Briton had a family that loved him and laid his body to rest in the cave. He states that this burial introduced to Briton the culture that radiated from the River Nile and the North African coast. The body being covered in a red substance is very significant to us. The Nubians of northeast Africa used this hue for symbolic reasons.

To create the now famous dark-red colour, the ancient Egyptian painter combined red ochre and oxide of iron with a vegetable gum binder. This red ochre was contracted from an iron ore called hematite. Recent discoveries have yielded evidence of iron ore mines in Swaziland and Zimbabwe dated to 27,000 B.C to 41,000 B.C.

Africans have been extracting and using hematite for thousands upon thousands of years.

The actual 'magic-religious' symbolism attached to the colour red may not have begun in Egypt but in Inner Africa. During the Palaeolithic (primitive) period 42,000 - 2000 B.C when Blacks invaded Europe, we find this act became a general practice. Soaking the body in this red substance was a sure sign of the African burial roots of Britain.[47]

Soviet scholars have pointed out that Central Africans have genetic connections to their ancestors. They spread from Europe into Asia. The African cultural practice of using red iron ore in burial customs soon evolved all over Europe and into the UK.

THE LAND THAT TIME FORGOT

Arthur Bryant 's book The Story of England explains that no other land of the same size has such a vast amount of scenery, soils and mineral deposits. At one time Britain's surface was the ocean's floor, at another a burning desert of rock with evidence of elephants and hippopotami.

To early Black settlers England became known as 'Tin Island'. The veins of tin and copper were formed by molten magma from submarine volcanoes. We have all been taught in school that the Romans were the first civilised people to 'discover' Britain; let's see what their writers say about this island of tin and the people who controlled and mined it.

In the first Century Romans called the island *Cassiterides*; a Latin word meaning Tin. The Romans believed that Tin Island is separated from Europe by the stormy channel and that a Black tribe known as the *Damnonii* occupied Cornwall.[48] This tribe kept their ancient customs and professed to have knowledge of the future.

Ancient European writers such as Dionysius Periegeta wrote that 'the rich sons of the noble Iberians (Blacks of Spain and Portugal)' dwelled on Tin Island, and the Roman writer Rufus Festus Avienus expressed that at the end of Europe lies the Hesperides (Britain), full of tin, "which the strong people of the Iberians occupy"[49]

The *Phoenicians* of North Africa were recorded to have visited Britain in ancient times. They were a great nation of navigators known to have crossed the Atlantic and planted a settlement in Florida.

They visited all western coasts of Europe trading with the metal workers of Cornwall and colonising some parts of Ireland. These Phoenicians were sent to the West on the bidding of their African Israelite leader king Solomon. It is during this period that the seal of Solomon was carved on the stones throughout Scotland.

The Black predecessors of the present British race were mining metals and iron ore in England since the dawn of history. They were the original 'Smiths' of Britain. They were the Black Smiths - Blacksmiths - a smith being a person who works with metals. The name 'Smith' is now the most common surname in England due to these early Black workers.

EARLY BLACK TRIBES OF BRITAIN

Around 6000 years ago, from their base of operations in Spain - then called 'Iberian Ethiopia'[50] – the Iberians or Black Celts migrated east to the Caucasus Mountains in Russia and west to the British Isles. When they arrived in England they brought with them the heiralpha, which was the ploughshare, used to till the earth.

To the Black Man the Earth was seen as being sacred. This is seen in the word *heiralpha*, from the words 'heir' meaning holy and 'alpha' meaning one.[51] They met other Blacks that brought with them agricultural sciences, tool making, pottery making and mining technologies of iron, copper, silver and salt.

These Black Iberians were deeply devoted to strong family ties and loved to pass their leisure time in singing and dancing. They spoke a tongue related to Egyptian and Cushite.[52]

David Mac Ritchie says these Iberians were spread all over the British Islands and some of their tribes were known as Damnonii and Silures. In the Illustrated Dictionary of British History it says of the Silures:

"A war like tribe, described by Tacticus (Roman Historian and Orator, 55AD to120AD) as swarthy and curly haired. They were persistently hostile to Rome and defeated Roman invading legions."

The word 'swarthy' comes from the German word 'schwarz' meaning 'black'. These were the types of people the Romans met with their coming to England. According to Skene, the powerful tribe of the Damnonii was the chief of those that lived on the marshland.

Pliny (a Roman writer, 23AD to 79 AD) characterises their complexion as aethiopium, that is, as black as an Ethiopian.[53] The Iberians were bearded and they worshipped the gods. Both men and women believed that they had knowledge of the future.

They had colleges in an island near the coasts of Brittany. These knowledgeable men and women (druids) who also professed to be able to control the forces of nature dressed in black gowns. Today we see university lecturer's, professors and barristers dressed in the same attire of black gowns passed on from these early Black druids.[54]

THE BLACKAMOORS OF BRITAIN

The British government insists that school children must study certain basic historical milestones such as 1066 and the Norman's invasion and the medieval period in order that they know and respect European culture and achievements.

Well, I believe every child in Britain should study the Moors in order to understand and respect Black culture and achievements.

However, they will not be taught about the Moors in the state killing fields (schools).

First, let us look at the word 'Moor'. As explained in the <u>Everyman's Encyclopaedia</u>, the word 'Moor' indicates the African origins of the aforementioned.

The Moors gave their name to the country we call 'Morocco'. Further, the word 'Mauri' means 'dark' or 'black'. The Moors were comprised of various African peoples such as Numidians, Phoenicians and Arabs, and the Moors of Spain was largely an African race.

In <u>Skeates Etymological Dictionary</u> it states that the word 'Moor' is a corruption of the word 'blackamoor' (as Black as a Moor). All Latin dictionaries will tell you that 'Maurus' or 'Mauri' means any dark or Black person; in Spanish it is 'Moros' which also means 'black'. Shakespeare uses 'Moor' as a synonym (the same word) for the word Black: In Shakespeare's <u>Othello</u> the principal character, *Othello*, is a Black Moor.

Why are Moors so important when we study the history of Britain? As pointed out in the introduction of this book, if you want to hide anything from Black people, they say, put it in a book. When we read about the early Roman victories in Britain, modern scholars seem, by a strange coincidence, to overlook or delete from their writings very significant points made by the Romans.

In reciting the victories in Britain the Roman general Theodosius Claudian wrote,

"He subdued the nimble blackamoors, not wrongly named the painted people". [55]

The Romans called the early Britons 'blackamoors'. The Moors' were invaded by various German tribes. These tribes later crossed into Britain from mainland Europe and destroyed or stole the Moors' land, culture and wealth. The invading Germans controlled the sea and trade routes and the Moors (Blacks) were killed, pushed out into the swamplands or integrated.

As time went on the swamplands that the Moors were pushed onto became known as the 'moors' or 'moorlands'.[56]

Thus the word moor suggests a great deal more than just the skin colour. When we look in the dictionary the word 'moor' also means 'swampland' or 'marshes'. The word moor has a lot in common with the Ugrian word 'kara' or 'ciar' as both these words also mean not only, black but also low, fertile or boggy land.

From the words 'kara' and 'ciar' we arrive at the English words 'carse', 'cerse', 'cress' and 'grass'. All these words relate to meadow or grasslands. This is the outcome of when the Blacks controlled the meadows i.e. Karr's Land or Moors Land.[57]

Many early scholars wrote that 'moor' is linked to the Latin words 'mare', 'meer', 'mor' or 'muir'. All these words mean the ocean itself. These names have come to represent the association between the sea and the nation of Black sea rovers and ancient navigators.

A NAME IS WORTH MOOR THAN GOLD

The Bible says, "A good name is worth more than gold" and a name liveth for evermore.

These statements are especially true when we are dealing with a people who have been robbed of the knowledge of self. We must understand that as detectives of Black history a name is a vital clue to leading us into deeper truths of the presence of Black people in ancient Europe and the British Isles.

Many names indicate the race of the people to which they belong. Let us look at some examples we find in Britain and examine their roots.

MOOR

In the last chapter we looked at the word 'moor' and how it means black skinned. Moor has been a long-standing surname in Britain with many variations such as Moore e.g. the actor, Roger Moore.

We have names such as 'Maurice', 'Morris' and 'Maureen', which are all linked to the great Moorish people of the past. Another English word from this root is 'Murray', meaning dark red or copper coloured; 'Murrey' and 'Murray' are common surnames in Britain.

One of the estates of this clan bore the significant name of 'The Black Barony'. Mr Skene expressed that the now famous location of Loch Ness was the centre of a district he calls "Moray".

Indeed these old traditional surnames gives us strong evidence that Black people inhabited Britain thousands of years before our parents came from the Caribbean in the 1950s and 1960s.

GREEN AND GORM

'Green' and 'Gorm' are rooted in *maurus* (moor). 'Gorm' is found attached to the names of Highland (and other) chiefs and kings of Britain. This word is given in Gaelic dictionaries as signifying 'blue' and 'green'. Thus, a man stained in what appears to be a blue-black or green-black skin.

CAIRENN, CAIREANN, KIRWAN, KAREN, KARAN

These are all borrowed from the Latin word 'Carina', taken from 'Carr' meaning black. These names are very common in Ireland. The best-known bearer of the name was *Cairenn Chasdubh*, (Cairen of the Black Curly Hair).

The origin of the name 'Kirwan' goes back to the Heremon of the Milesians, a people who probably came from Spain. In Irish their name is 'Ciardubhain' (black).

We must remember that in ancient times, Spain was also called Iberia Ethiopia due to the fact the people living there were identical to the Africans. Variations of the above include **'Cera'**, **'Ceara'** which means red skinned. This was one of the names of the wives of Nemed, the legendary invader of Ireland.

CIAR, CIARA, KARA, CIARAN

These words mean black. In Ireland many of the saints bore the above names. The best known is *St. Ciara of Kilkeary* and *Ciaran of Seir Kieran*, County Offaly.

DONN, DUNCAN, DONNCHADD

These are all compounds of the word 'donn' meaning 'brown skinned' and also the 'brown lord'. In Ireland a common variation is 'Donnfhlaidh' or 'Dunflaith' meaning 'brown princess'. The English variation is 'Dunla'. Although the name 'Dunnes' has ties to England it is commonplace in Ireland.

DONOVAN

This pedigree goes back to a 10th century King of Munster. From his son, *Donnabhain*, came the family name, ('donn' meaning brown and 'dubhann' meaning black). They were a part of a noble race in Mui (Ireland).

DOYLE, DOUGAL, DOUGLAS, DUBGALL, DUFFY

These names are common all over the UK; they are extremely prevalent in the South-East of Britain particularly around Wexford. These names mean, literally, the 'black man' or 'black foreigner'. In the <u>Dictionary of Irish Mythology</u> by Peter B Ellis, we are told that there was a druidess by the name of *Dubh* (Black). She was slain by her husband Enna by a slingshot where upon she fell into a pool. The Celtic word for pool is 'linn'. Thus the pool became known as 'Dubh's Pool' or 'Dubhlinn'. This, it is said, is how *Dublin* the capital city of Ireland achieved its name, after the Black druidess.

GORMAN

This was a common British name in ancient times. It means 'black' or 'swarthy'. As late as the 7th century there was a Black king of Ireland by the name of King Gorman. A very popular name amongst ancient Irish princesses was 'Gormlaith', which means 'blue black princess' or the 'illustrious princess'.

BLAKE

This name is common both to Wales, England and Ireland. The name first entered into Wales.

'Blake' is a corruption of the word 'black'. The original Blakes (blacks) were known for the dark hue of their skin. The Blakes settled in Galway City and county where, for hundreds of years, they were rich landowners and merchants. Many of them were mayors and sheriffs of the city. They built castles, some of which still stand today. Apart from being statesmen they were also soldiers who went to battle in the crusades and also took part in the Irish uprisings.

THE LAST BLACK KING OF BRITAIN

As discussed in earlier chapters, there were several nations or tribes of Aboriginal Blacks residing in the UK. They had set up separate kingdoms that flourished during prehistoric times.

With the arrival of the Europeans around 2700 B.C – during two major waves of incursions – the original people were pushed to the swamplands and hills or intermarried.

However not all the Black kingdoms were wiped out totally. For example, we see that as late as the tenth century there was a Black King of Scotland.

History knows him as 'Kenneth', sometimes 'Dubh' or 'Niger'. Irish books call him *Kenneth of the three Black divisions*. According to the old historians, Scotland (also known as Alban) was split into seven divisions.[58] This king evidently ruled over three of the divisions that were still predominately Black.

These divisions remained Black and intact despite the White divisions around them. History has it that the Black king was constantly at war with a leader known as *Fionn* ('the White'). Fionn eventually wins and drives him out for at least 20 years.

A son of King Kenneth or 'Dubh' known too as 'Kenneth Mac Dubh' regained the kingship for his father in the year 997, reigning until 1004. His son was also termed 'Donn' or 'brown'. The fact that 'Donn' implies a lighter shade than 'Duh' may allow one to draw the conclusion that Donn had a white mother.[59]

THE BLACK VIKINGS OF DENMARK

Have you ever heard of the Black Huns? The answer to this question is most likely "NO!" History lessons in our schools seem to have a very neat way of hiding or sweeping under the carpet of ignorance whole segments of people and nations. The history of Denmark needs to be taught in schools because Denmark had a direct major impact on British history.

Many centuries before Attila the Hun, the provinces of Rome were invaded by hordes of barbarians. One segment of the barbarians was the Cimbri. They were described as ancient Germans. The Cimbri were also known by a second name *Dani* i.e. 'the Danes', hence we have the name Denmark.

They occupied present day Denmark. They were described as having huge shoulders and swarthy (black) skin. They were known to be a warlike people that courageously fought against the Romans. History knows them as the Black Huns.[60]

It is reasonable to ask, "Where are these Black Huns today?" Because when we look at Denmark today we see the fair skinned, blond haired and blue-eyed Europeans who have nothing in common with the original Dani. The answer lies in the Norwegians and Finns.

The original Danes were invaded and put to flight by the Norwegians (Normans or North men) who were fair skinned barbarians from Northern Europe and also the Finns of Finland.

The very word 'Finn' or 'Find' means 'white' hence Finland means the 'white land'.[61]   The Black Danes were driven out of Denmark.

However in historic times they took to the seas to find new domains to conquer.   It is probable that the majority of the Vikings belonged to these Black Scandinavians

In the book <u>Irish Names for Children</u> by Laurence Flanagan, he says that the names Douglas, Dougal and Dubghall mean 'black foreigner'.   It was applied by the Irish to the Vikings, particularly the Danes in 850 A.D; thus we read in history books that the Danes or Danish people plundered England, Scotland, Wales and Ireland but what they fail to let us know is the racial origin of these invaders.

Scottish writers say of these Danish invaders that they were of dark complexion, deformed in their appearance; they had flat noses, broad shoulders, and were bearded with a shrilled voice.   They attained great power and were able to enforce a mail (tax payment) on the British people.

This payment became know as 'blackmail,' 'black' because of the army demanding the tax and the word 'mail' means payment. The origin of this term was 'Dane-gelt' and later became 'blackmail'. In the fifth century the Danes were able to levy this tax annually even in Rome.

Today the word blackmail means a forced payment to a villain in order to protect you from harm or injury.[62]

The Irish call all strangers to their land 'galls'. Every since the Danes or Dubhgaills (black strangers) came to Ireland there has been a battle with the Finngaills or white strangers for superiority. In 877 a battle took place where the Finngaills won.

The Danes were driven out of Ireland to Scotland.

Some scholars mistakenly try to mislead others by saying that the designations of black and white referred to hair colour; however this reasoning is futile.[63]

Danish people today are not known for having black hair in fact they're known for the very opposite and we have many written historical testimonies stating that the colours represented skin colour.

One such example is given by St. Berchan of Ireland. When speaking of his fellow white Norwegians he calls them, "gentiles of pure colour" and says that "the Danes were not of pure colour, they were dubh, black".[64]

The designation by common people of one race to another is almost always founded upon some physical distinction and the most common is skin complexion. In America for example it was the Red Indians and the Pale-faced Europeans.

Throughout the British Isles the Danes were also known as the Black heathens and this surely was not due to their hair colour.

From the perspective of Blacks' involvement in British history, William the Conqueror is important because the Norman invasion that he led in 1066 put an end to the Black Danes in Britain.

Chapter 5

Remnants of a long lost culture

THE ORIGINAL ROOTS ROCKERS

Youth music culture and urban culture today is another way of saying Black culture. Wherever we may be on this Planet, the one thing that Black people have in common is our love of rhythm and beat. We teach the world how to dance and stay in rhythm with the sound waves. And it was the Blacks of ancient times that gave the people of Britain their very first dancing lesson.

It is interesting that the most common and well-known traditional dance of old England is traced back to the Black Man of Asia (Earth).

We have all seen those old Technicolor films on Sunday afternoons showing Robin Hood, his merry men and Maid Marian dancing in the woods with light hops and leaps and bells around their ankles.

We have also seen pictures of those quaint country folks at English festivals and May Day games with little sticks in their hands which they knock together, doing a similar dance where they leap and prance around and we think, 'How quintessentially English this is!' Is it not strange that the most traditional dance of this country is called the *Morris Dance* sometimes spelt 'morrice', 'mourice', 'mores' or 'moorish' dance? [65]

The Morris Dance is seen as the national dance of England yet England has never been a part of Morocco during historic times. Nor is this dance the property of Morocco. It is peculiarly English.[66] It is a well-known fact that dancing is second nature to African (Blackamoors) people. Hence, this may hint at the role that Black people living in England had in bringing this dance into being.

Historians differ as to when this dance lesson was introduced to England. David MacRitchie says this dance was here during prehistoric times when the original man inhabited these shores. Others say that the Morris or Moorish dance has its origin in Spain amongst the Blackamoors, and it was originally a military dance of the moors introduced during the reign of Edward III.

THE BLACK AND WHITE MINSTREL SHOW

When I was growing up, I remember every Sunday watching the *Black and White Minstrel Show* on BBC1. The show was so traditionally old English and yet the characters were European men painting their faces and hands black and wearing black woolly wigs singing 'Mammy'. I had no idea that this was telling me of the long lost Black nation of Britain.

Sir Walter Scott indicates the existence in Britain of a considerable black population in historical times.[67] They formed a recognised part of a class of wandering minstrels. These people were always linked to magic, which was known as the 'black art'.

They undertook a peculiar dance once known as the *Black-Almain*, which may be nothing more than a variation of the Morris Dance performed by their forefathers.[68] They were also the earliest rappers in Europe. They would travel the countryside as bairds telling stories of old and magical times in perfect rhyme.

These wandering Black tribes of performers were largely shunned by the white inhabitants and were called *gypsies*. The word 'gypsy' is literally a corruption of the word *Egypt* or *Egyptian* (African).[69]

The gypsies were traditionally known for casting spells, witchcraft and having the ability to read people's palms or crystal balls in order to tell the future. Could this be a remnant of the high cultured civilisation from which they came?

This swarthy, nomadic race possesses the same characteristics as the Black jugglers and dancers. At times they were called 'Moors', 'Tartars', 'Danes' and 'Saracens'. Their skills and arts were developed into circuses.

We can still see the racial characteristics in the large earrings, gay colours, and oily plaited hair of the performers and the half 'Salaams' with which the circus acrobats greet each other.[70]

There is probably no pure-blooded gypsy tribe today due to intermarrying over the decades. However they are still generally swarthy and their hair is generally black, greasy and plaited.

They were the foundation for the sport of boxing in Europe. At their gatherings it was very common to see wrestling matches and bare knuckling boxing. They were the top prize-fighters of their day. These gypsies and travellers are today shunned and in themselves shun British society.

When many of our parents came in the 40s and 50s they saw signs on public houses saying:

"No Blacks, Irish or Gypsies".

BRING IN THE CLOWNS

It is the common practice in history that a conquered people will sink from the position of dreaded foes to that of servants, jesters, wandering players and buffoons.

We see that the tribes of North America, once so terrible to Europeans, have fallen to a level where they are used today as entertainers in holiday resorts dressed as rain dancers prancing around a pole.

The Aborigines of Australia entertain their European Governors and guests with their ancient games, customs and ritual displays.

Most of our so-called Afro American global movie stars come from a comedy background: Chris Rock, Eddie Murphy, Richard Pryor and Bill Cosby are to name just a few. Their ancestors used to put fear into the enemy but now are reduced to making 'the enemy' laugh.

This has also happened in Ancient Britain. A once proud nation was made into a race that fooled around like monkeys. In the words 'clown' and 'buffoon' we are seeing remnants of this once noble Black people.

Just picture a clown. Even when we see a white man playing a clown he still has to paint his face white. This is because after generations of being bred out they could not find any Black men to paint their face white.

Originally the face had to be painted white because the clown was Black. Over this white paint they would show features of that subject people - the cheeks and head would be painted red, depicting the *Redskins*, as were the forehead and between the eyes which is reminiscent of *Hindus*.

They would try to paint around the lips to give the effect of 'blubber' lips. To complete the Black effect they would wear Afro wigs of strange and grotesque fashion.[71]

The very words 'clown' and 'buffoon' originally meant a man of 'brutal make up'.[72] This was the sentiment felt towards these people. This is sentiment is also reflected in the British language in which the word Black signifies everything evil, ugly and grotesque in life, as demonstrated below:

1. *Black day:* a bad day; *to be blackened;* to have a bad character

2. *Blackguard:* a scoundrel

3. *Black market:* illegal goods and services

Chapter 6

Who built Stonehenge?

What is Stonehenge? The word Stonehenge comes from the Old English word 'hengen' which means 'that which is hung up'. Stonehenge is the most famous prehistoric monument in Britain.

It is a great circle of standing, lintel (horizontal) stones which can be found on the Salisbury Plain in Wiltshire. Stonehenge has attracted scientists and specialists from all over the world. This one monument has proven to be a major archaeological mystery to the European race.

According to studies, the site is a sacred spot devoted to worship and, in a sense, is been comparable to the structure of a cathedral. Christopher Chippindale in the book Who owns Stonehenge? says that this ancient ruin is over 4000 years old.

From the ground, Stonehenge can seem a confusion of stones, standing and laying, whole and broken. Some stones are now missing or have been taken away to make bridges or build dams, but the basic plan is straightforward enough.

The outer circle consists of thirty grey stone blocks weighing a fascinating 50 tons each and standing thirteen and half feet tall, measuring a collective diameter of 97 feet. A continuous circle of smaller slabs was placed and joined on top of them. Investigations have shown that these sockets and joints indicating a very advanced technology precisely connect the construction.

The inner circles consisted of about 60 blue stones and within this diameter were two horseshoe shaped set of stones, one inside the other, and opening towards the northeast. In the middle of the inner horseshoe was a flat 16-foot sandstone altar.

A huge marker stood 80 yards east of the alter set in such a way as to cast a shadow on the alter at dawn on the day of the summer solstice. These slabs signify the places on the celestial horizon where the sun and the moon rise and set.[73]

Stonehenge also acts as an excellent astronomical calendar of which the seasons of the year and the eclipses of the sun and the moon could be accurately predicted.

In 1963 Gerald S. Hawkins of the Smithsonian Astrophysical Observatory calculated the directions of the lines joining various stones, and using an electronic computer found a remarkable correlation between the directions of the lines and the direction of the rising and setting of the sun and moon. The chances of such correlation being coincidental are about one in one hundred million.[74]

Another amazing fact about Stonehenge is that some of the gigantic stones used were not native to that area. The stones are only found in Western Wales, which is a staggering 300 miles away. Somehow they had to be carried there and one must ask the questions, why and how?[75]

We have been misled into believing that no one knows who built Stonehenge. The truth is that they have known the builders for many years. The British are well known for being meticulous (very precise about details). They would never have a monument the size of Stonehenge and be satisfied with not knowing who built it. One thing for sure is that they know THEY didn't build it.

The scientific scholars know whom the owners and builders are but hide this truth, as it would destroy the lie that the first Blacks came to England during the 1940s.

The absolute truth is that the Asiatic (Earth) Black Man and Woman are the owners and builders of Stonehenge. British scholars would rather say that the details of those who built Stonehenge cannot be traced, than admit that Black people were the wisest builders on the earth. This long lost Black nation of aboriginal Britons left a testimony of their advanced civilisation - something those later generations could look at and marvel.

The English historian, Gerald Massey says that Stonehenge was built by a Black architect named Morien from Egypt. Brother Reverend Barashango states that around "2,800 B.C a group of Black cyclopean (a pre classical Greek way of masonry) builders came to England".

These people were descendants of the original rulers of the planet Earth whom J. A. Rogers calls 'Cushites' from which he says derived the terminology Celts. These Black Celts built the gargantuan structure of Stonehenge.[76]

Reverend Barashango and J. A. Rogers are not alone in their assumption. In the 1800's, the learned Scottish scholar Godfrey Higgins expressed the view in his essay <u>Celtic Druids</u> that,

"A great Black nation called Celtae of whom the Druids were the priest, spread themselves all over the whole earth. They are to be traced in their rude gigantic monuments from India to the extremity of Britain".[77]

Higgins, states the learned scholar Maurice, says that 'Cushites', i.e. Celts, built the great temples in India and Britain. While the learned mathematician, Reuben Burrow has no hesitation in pronouncing Stonehenge to be "a temple of the black, curly-headed Buddha". The religion of Buddha, of India, is well known to have been very ancient.

In the most ancient temples scattered throughout Asia, where worship is still continued today, the most ancient Buddha's found have jet black flat faces, thick lips and curly hair.[78]

When one looks at the hair on the head of these Buddha's they will remind you of present-day Black people. Blacks have a very old hairstyle that is distinctly African and can be see on Egyptian art in their temples. Even though this hairstyle is exclusive to Blacks we call it *China Bumps* - now we know why!

The Buddha had an immense empire that scholars know reached into Britain.

In the old books of the Hindus (Indians), we meet with accounts of great battles that took place between the followers of the *Linga* and those of the *Ioni*, and that the latter were expelled from India under the name of *Yavanas*.

The Yavanas (Buddhists) priests were known as *Culdees* and *Jaines*. They were pushed out to the West. On their way it is written that they built in the city of Babylon, *Colchis* (home of the Golden Fleece in Jason and the Argonauts) and the city of Iona called afterwards Gaza (Palestine).

They went on to build Athens and Troy. They claim to have also carried the religion of *Osiris* and *Isis* into Egypt. They took the Deity *Janus* (from which comes the word January) into Italy where their followers were called *Ombri*. They found the city of Rome and built the temple of Isis now called Notre Dame or the Queen of Heaven, at Paris. They built Stonehenge, or 'Ambres-stan' and *Avebury* or *Ambrespore*.[79]

These Ancient Black Buddha's professed a religion called *Om*. Many scholars write that Black people practised this religion of peace all over the earth at one time.

The Buddhist priests found Oxford on the river which they called Isis and Cambridge on the river 'Cam', 'Cham', 'Ham', 'Am' or 'Om'.

According to Godfrey Higgins they found a college like Oxford or Cambridge, which remained until the Reformation (16th century), when its library (probably the oldest in the world at that time) was dispersed or destroyed. It is known that parts of the library went to Douay in Flanders.[80]

The Buddhist priests built 'Iseur' or 'Oldborough' or 'Aldborough' (the ancient capital of England), and called the Yorkshire River by the name 'Om-ber' or 'Umber' or 'Humber' (Humberside) after the religion of Om. They called the capital of the state of *Iseur, Brigantia ,* which is the same name as the state they (WHO?) had left behind in Iberia (Spain).

OTHER STONE CIRCLES

Avebury:

According to the <u>Encyclopaedia Britannica</u> an excess of 600 structures of various materials and sizes - yet similar in formation to Stonehenge - have been discovered in England and Western France.

One of the largest ceremonial sites in prehistoric Europe is Avebury. This henge monument covers a staggering 29 acres. The great circle of Avebury has 100 stones; two smaller internal stone circles were added during the Beaker period (2000 - 1700 BC). It had an avenue of standing stones leading to the *Sanctuary*, another circle over a mile distant.

The great Scottish Historian David Mac Ritchie has no doubt that these stone circles are evidence of a dark skinned people who inhabited Europe and especially Britain in former times. Stone circles can be found in all countries where dark skinned people are.

Tasmania

Tasmania has its stone circles and cairns and Scotland shows the presence of the same work and the same people.

Australian Deccan

In the Australian Deccan there are dolmens and stone circles as in Britain and Europe.

Borneo

In the jungle of one part of Borneo there is a great area known to the Malays as Fallan Batoe "The Field of Stone". It contains rocking stones, standing stones and other stones.

British Guiana

In British Guiana there are many stone circles. They are covered with marks and curious picture writings that resemble the marks found on the stones in Borneo. The present inhabitants know nothing of their origin.

North America

In Wyoming, built by the indigenous inhabitants, we have the Bighorn Medicine wheel. The

Aborigine, for astronomical, reasons used this wheel.

On many of these monuments are inscribed the journey of the *celestial spheres*, the *path of the constellations*, the *cycle of the seasons* and many other scientific insignia.

At the same time that Stonehenge and Avebury were being built their 'classmates' in Egypt, 6000 miles away, were building similar stone monuments - the pyramids. Thus we have in the East the triangular shape being utilised and in the West the circular shape.

When we put together the western circle and the eastern triangle i.e. the 360-degree circle with a pyramid within its circumference and the *All Seeing Eye of Osiris*, we get the symbol used by the African priests in the Kemetic (Egyptian) mystery school system.

This is the same symbol used by European secret societies ruling the planet today. You will find symbol on the American dollar bill, which was designed by Freemasons.

Chapter 7

The very dark ages

THE BIRTH OF THE ROMAN EMPIRE

We earlier mentioned how the Greeks became the first civilised White people in the known world. They benefited tremendously from the Cretan/Egyptian knowledge, wisdom and understanding and used that knowledge to colonise large areas of the Mediterranean and the so-called Middle East.

Two hundred years later the Greeks were replaced by the very thick headed Romans.
The Romans combined the knowledge that they had been receiving from the Greeks with their military nature. They soon overran the Greeks and Greece itself became a Roman Province. Rome used its superior war machine and military might to overcome the Mediterranean area, North Africa and the so-called Middle East. Thus began the Roman Empire.[81]

This should be a lesson to all Black students: While Black civilisations produced a far superior, highly cultured way of life we neglected the science of warfare. Our wisdom was used primarily for spiritual and religious progress; however we negated to place ourselves in a position that would allow us to protect that which we owned.

ROME GETS AN AFRICAN EMPEROR

Septimius Severus is a name our youth need to know more about. He was a true 'soul brother' who made it to the top of white man's world. Septimius was born in Libya, northeast Africa. Ishakamusa Barashango tells us that he was born in an upper middle class family on April 11th, 146 AD.

He received a Latin education but kept a strong African accent. By the age of 26 he obtained a seat in the Roman Senate and rose to the rank of Senior Magistrate. He went to Spain and became a governor and then the Consular. A consular is an elected magistrate who jointly holds the highest authority in that country.

Septimus then marched on Rome and defeated all pretenders to the Roman throne. He became the Emperor of Rome, an essentially white nation. He improved conditions for soldiers, and offered new career opportunities to provincial Romans. Throughout the whole of his spectacular rise he never forgot his roots.

He gave strict orders that his food be transported from Africa. His top officials were African and he wanted semi home rule for his African homeland.[82]

Now what I am about to explain every person in England needs to know, especially if you are of colour. It was this Black Emperor that visited England in 197 AD and brought order to the land.

When he arrived in the UK he was seen as the 'Messiah' and the 'Deliverer'. He drove many pillaging German tribes back across the English Channel.

He divided Britain into two provinces and stopped the Scottish tribes from raiding England. Septimius establish what became known as the century of peace in Britain.[83]

Septimius travelled to Africa in 202 AD and studied in the Nile Valley schools of Ancient Egyptian wisdom. He was known as a zealous student and left nothing unturned.

In 208 He returned to Britain and found the city of York, which at that time was England's capital. He died whilst at York at the age of 64 from pneumonia.

Up to this very day one of the greatest Roman Emperor's is buried at York and hardly anyone knows he is there.[84]

I ask you dear reader, is this the way we should honour our past legends?

HELLS ANGELS WREAK HAVOC IN EUROPE

During the Roman domination of Europe and North Africa the Romans were continually defending themselves from the barbarous German tribes. The Germans were well known for their dirty, vulgar and violent behaviour. The Greeks named them 'Germans', which literally means the 'man of many germs'.[85]

In 395 AD these onslaughts began to threaten the existence of Rome itself. Rome had to call back all its legions to defend its capital and homeland. Among these Germans there were some who were extremely savage, such as the *Ostrogoths, Visigoths, Saxons* and *Jutes.*

However, the most ruthless and demonic tribe was the ultra destructive *Vandals*. They demolished anything and everything in sight. It was as if they were designed to destroy for absolutely no reason at all.

To remind us of how good they were at utter mindless destructive behaviour, we still use the term 'vandalism' and 'vandal' in contemporary English language to describe the same conduct.

It must be noted that it was these same Germans - Vandals - who reached North Africa and wrecked our civilisations to a point where some have been wiped out of total memory.[86]

Europe, under these mainly German tribes, fell into spiritual and mental darkness; hence the term 'the dark ages' - sometimes called the medieval period. The old masters of Europe, the Greeks and Romans, were no longer able to keep Europe mentally and spiritually alive with the African knowledge that was learnt or stolen down the centuries.

Chapter 8

Behold I will place you in a strange land for 400 years

THE RENAISSANCE – THE DOOR, THE WAY AND THE BLACK LIGHT

In 570 AD a man by the name of Muhammad was born in Mecca, Arabia. This one man was set to change the destiny of man and mankind.

Muhammad was chosen by God to bring back that old time religion that was now lost to the world. He taught that there was only one God and humanity should be in submission to that God. This religion was named Islam (submission).

Muhammad brought a new emphasis to religion, one of learning. The first commandment given to Muhammad from his Creator was to read. Reading and learning became the central tenants of this faith.

Islam began to spread from Arabia into Africa. It reached North Africa and caused a mental and spiritual revolution amongst a people called Moors.

They accepted this faith with such zeal that they created a Muslim empire that was to change Europe forever. [87]

Reverend Barashango explains that in 711 these African Muslims, with their Arab brothers and led by their African leader Gebel Tarik, left Africa and travelled to Europe. They landed on the rock named in honour of Gebel Tarik. We now call the rock Gibraltar.

Today there is a major diplomatic row over this rocky land piece between the Governments of Britain and Spain, both however forgetting the African roots of this rock. Here Gebel Tarik built a mighty fortress from which he defeated all the German Goths and made the Moors the masters of Spain.

He conquered Europe all the way to Southern France. These Black and Arab Muslims gave the backward Europeans one of the finest cultures Europe ever had. Western society loves to remind us all how vast the Roman Empire was, yet this great Moorish empire included more land than the Roman Empire in its heyday. [88]

On the 27th of October 1993, Prince Charles gave a lecture at Oxford University and he reminded the wise scholars of Oxford of the debt that the West owed to these Black Moors. He went on to explain how these Moors controlled and civilised Europe for 800 years, from the eighth to the fifteenth century.

The Moors introduced and expanded the sciences of astronomy, mathematics, algebra, law, history, medicine, pharmacology, optics, agriculture, architecture, theology, and music to name but a few.

Prince Charles went on to say that many of the traits that Europe prides itself on came from the Moors of Spain - diplomacy, free trade, open borders, universities, academic research techniques of anthropology, etiquette, fashion, various types of medicine and hospitals came from them.[89]

One of the most important introductions of the Moors to Europe was the Arabic numerals system i.e. 1,2,3 – you know – the numbers one to ten that we use everyday.

The Moors had to explain the very concept of zero, which was a very arduous task for Europeans to grasp, having been used to the

Roman numerals I, V, X etc, which makes arithmetic near impossible.

What was even more remarkable was how tolerant these Moors were. Even though the Blackamoors were the new masters in town *they allowed Christians and Jews freedom to practice their religion and their inherited beliefs*. [90]

The Moors reintroduced to Europe the quest and thirst for learning. Eight hundred years of this African Wisdom pouring into Europe led to the birth of 'the Renaissance' - a French word, which means to be awakened or renewed. Europe was now ready to rise.

Before the coming of the Blackamoors there was no such thing as chivalry or stately court life among the aristocracy. Prince Charles' speech to Oxford stated that in the tenth century the Muslims had lending libraries when the English King, King Alfred was still eating human flesh at his dining table. One Muslim ruler had over 400,000 books in his own personal library - more books than the rest of non-Muslim Europe put together. [91]

J.A. Rogers says that while the Moorish Kings were living in magnificent palaces, the kings of

France, England and Germany had homes little better than stables - windowless and chimneyless, with a hole in the roof for smoke to escape.

From the main power bases of the Blackamoors in Europe, Spain, Italy and Portugal, their Black blood penetrated into the royal families of Europe. Colonel W. H. Turton traced the ancestry of Elizabeth, daughter of Edward IV of England, and the mother of Henry VIII and found several Moorish kings, an Arab born in Mecca, a Moorish ex-slave named Mujahid and Leon, a Black Jew.[92]

The portrait of Queen Charlotte Sophia, consort of George III, by Ramsay, clearly shows the Black features. Indeed noted Englishmen wrote about how her nostrils and mouth spread too wide.[93]

BITING THE HAND THAT FEEDS YOU

Europe had a very strange way of thanking their African Saviours for bringing them back into civilisation. The Black Man in his 800-year victory over Europe was in fact laying the foundations for his own defeat and destruction.

After sharing African supreme wisdom and opening mental, spiritual and scientific doors that Europeans had never dreamed of before, the Europeans felt it was time to fight for their own independence and rid the Blackamoors from their lands.

The Blackamoors' power began to decline in the 13th century and they started to lose control over their European lands. In 1492, King Ferdinand and Queen Isabella of Spain drove out the last of the Moors from Spain and sent them packing back to Africa. It was a true case of biting the hand that feeds you.[94]

During this period Spain and Portugal - due to the opulent and learned presence of the Blackamoors - were the first among their European brethren to establish strong central governments. After learning from Blackamoors that the earth was not flat but round, these two nations set to the seas.

On 3rd of August 1492, Christopher Columbus a half-black, half-Jewish Italian set sail from Palos in Spain. The King and Queen of Spain commissioned him to 'discover', exploit and colonise new lands. His navigator who made it all possible was a Blackamoor by the name of Niger.

This voyage was to change the world forever. Columbus discovered what we mislabel and call today America and the West Indies. Soon the floodgates of Europe were open.

Columbus as we now know 'discovered' nothing new (Read chapter 2 on *Ancient America*). Soon European nations were trampling over each other to invest in similar colonial ventures.

It is written in numerous books and diaries of that time that when the Europeans sailed to the islands, the Indian girls would swim out to their ships and greet them with the greeting words of peace "tainos".[95]

Little did they know that with the European came a new strange way of life to the natives, that of cruelty, torture and enslavement. Their lands were taken right from beneath their feet and they were made to toil under an unbearable burden. It must be noted that the number one export out of Europe was not science or technology but diseases.

The Indians of the so-called West Indies have a recorded history extending over 16,000 years in that region of the world. When Christopher Columbus arrived he stated that the islands were well populated. However there are virtually no indigenous Caribbean-Indians surviving today.

The Indians of the West Indies and North and South America died like flies from slavery, wars and diseases.

Lets look at a typical example: There were over 100,000 Arawak Indians living on the Island of Jamaica when Columbus arrived on 5th May 1494. He went to investigate reports of gold on 'Xamayca', now called Jamaica (the land of wood and water). He wrote that it was the fairest isle that eyes ever beheld; the land seemed to touch the sky. There was no gold so he left.[96]

The Spaniards returned in 1510 and within 100 years they were successful in wiping out virtually the whole population who had been living there for thousands of years before.

Europe based their economies on agricultural products that required intensive labour. They needed the exotic and mineral wealth from these lands but were not willing to work the lands for themselves.

They required slaves to plant and harvest sugar, tobacco and coffee. These new super slaves had to be strong and virile and able to work virtually non-stop every day of the week.

1555 – THE WORST CRIME IN HISTORY

The British felt very envious of the new wealth gained by Spain and other Mediterranean countries. It had become well known that the Portuguese had found tall and strong Black men in Africa that were ideal for working their lands.

In 1555 Queen Elizabeth 1, sponsored John Hawkins to pioneer the African slave trade. John Hawkins was a ruthless and evil rogue, yet he was a master seaman for that time. He set sail from Plymouth in October between 1555 and 1562 in a ship named 'Jesus'.

He sailed to West Africa where he lived for some time. The Africans welcomed him and treated him as a brother and friend. He then took possession of 300 Africans, partly by sword and partly by tricks and lies.[97] This officially started the worst crime in world history.

Many of us have seen the Hollywood depiction of slavery in the film 'Roots'. This caused outrage in Black communities all over the world when first shown during the 1980s. Yet this was Hollywood's family viewing version of the slave trade. We can only but imagine the true horrors of slavery.

The Honourable Elijah Muhammad said if we were able to see the true horrors of slavery it would make a brass monkey shed tears. This wicked trade made England rich beyond belief.

It was these Africans - slaves - that put the 'Great' into Britain. The British supplied their colonies with Africans to work their lands. This brought a tremendous influx of wealth and capital.

However this wealth was to be eclipsed by the *Asiento Agreement* of 1713, signed by England and Spain. This agreement allowed Britain to supply Spain and her colonies with slaves from Africa for a staggering 30 years. England became the great slave trader of the world.[98]

Monies earned from the slave trade and the agricultural and mineral wealth from the West Indies and Africa were the very basis for the industrial revolution in Europe and built European cities into the superpowers that they are seen as today.

Due to wickedly wise mind control techniques and consistent brainwashing the very victims of the slave trade, Africans, are left feeling ashamed of slavery. We have nothing to feel ashamed of, as we were not the perpetrators but the victims.

We want to forget and forgive those who perpetrated this heinous crime without receiving so much as an apology. But we must *study* the slave trade - not from pure emotion - but from analytical research.

The Hidden Truth series will include a whole volume dedicated to the slave trade and its after effects. We will never understand the world today until we become experts on the effects of slavery on the African mind.

Every student of history regardless of their colour, nationality or creed must devote time to study slavery not from the view point of developing hatred but in order to understand the global economic world that we live in today.

THE ARAB SLAVE TRADE

The Arabs took advantage of regional wars in Africa to buy captives from the victors. They used the old but very successful divide and rule technique. They worked one group against the other and took and killed the best and strongest.

The Arabs during the 1400's began to raid the coastal towns of Mombassa in Kenya, Kilwa, Sofala and Mogadishu. They also ventured inland to what we call today Uganda, Malawi and Rwanda. These raids would be at nightfall, just as the villagers were having their communal dinner.[99]

The Arab slave trade was a ratio of two women to every man to fill the demand for concubines. This lopsided enslavement process contributed to the depopulation of Africa by siphoning off potential and actual mothers.

Slavery was not just the destruction of African manhood but also African womanhood.

From 1650 to 1900, Europe and Asia's population quadrupled (400%) while Africa's population increased by only 20%.

We must be clear that the Arab slave trade differed from the European slave trade in one important factor: The slaves were not considered purely as capital.

It was true that many Arabs saw Africans as inferior humans and lots of money was made from their capture, but this was done within the tributary economic framework. Many of the Arabs were indeed African themselves.

European chattel slavery was unique in the sense of the total disregard for any aspect of humanity.

THE NUMBERS GAME

What kind of numbers were involved in slavery? It is impossible to be certain. According to S. E. Anderson, a Professor of Mathematics, at least 10 million African women and 5 million men were sold in the Arab slave trade. Some 14 to 20 million African men, women and children were killed.[100]

According to other academics such as W. E. B. Dubois over 100 million Africans lost their lives just in the middle passage, i.e. the transporting of slaves from Africa to the West Indies and America.

According to social scientists, Africa had lost over 280 million of its population between 1650 and 1900.[101] Can we imagine the effect that would have on any continent? We must remember that the slave traders were not interested in kidnapping the meek and feeble.

They stole the young and strong. Among those captured were actual or potential farmers, priests, chemists, mathematicians, doctors, astronomers, artists, builders, engineers, inventors, economists and many more.

Slavery was worse than any atomic or hydrogen bomb being detonated. Africa was left devastated, crippled and decimated. The cream of the continent was taken to help build foreign powers that invested the money to rape Africa of its mineral wealth.

As if this was not enough, the children of those slave masters now say, "Why can't Africa and Africans get up and do for self and stop begging for world relief?"

Chapter 9

The forming of the Black Community in England

People believe that black people came to Britain only in 1945. Yet in the <u>Gentleman's Magazine</u> volume.34 printed in 1764, it showed that people were complaining that Negroes and Blackamoors were flooding London. At that time London only had a population of 675,000, which was made up of over 20,000 Blacks.

Africans became increasingly common in English towns. It became fashionable to employ African servants. Some people objected to these Africans' settlements. In 1596, Queen Elizabeth I, who pioneered the Africans to be enslaved, issued orders that they be expelled from Britain.

In 1601 a second Royal Proclamation was issued stating that all Blackamoors should be speedily evicted. Caspar van Senden was licensed to deport them. The proclamation was hand written by Queen Elizabeth herself.[102]

A FEW GOOD MEN

Cities like London, Bristol, Manchester, London and Cardiff were major slave holding and distributing centres.

The planters and merchants grew rich and fat. They owned many lavish estates overseas. Many of today's multinational companies made their wealth via the slave trade: Lloyds Underwriters insured slaves and the slave ships, P&O Ferries transported the slaves and Tate and Lyle were the plantation owners.

The people that suffered were the poor Africans who were captured and turned into slaves. They lost their names, culture, language, religion and traditions. They were now living a life of burden.

Their children, if they survived, were born into bondage and many died struggling for their freedom. It was common to read adverts in local and national newspapers, amongst *Fabrics to sell* and *Rooms to rent*, *Little Negro boys and girls for sale*. Also there were block advertisement bookings for runaway slaves to be returned to their masters.

In the early 1700s, slaves who were baptised as Christians were considering themselves free. Slave owners did not wish this practice to continue. They asked the Crown law officers, Yorke and Talbot for judgement. On 14th January 1729, the judgement was returned that slaves remained slaves whether Christian or not.[103]

Granville Sharp was one of very few white people who argued that Black people were not destined to be slaves. It is not true that Black people owe their freedom to Granville Sharp or any other white liberal, but we must give credit where credit is due.

Granville Sharp became involved in helping to abolish slavery by accident. He helped to legally free a young Black man, Jonathan Strong who had been beaten up and thrown out by his master then kidnapped again. Sharp was involved in the abolition of slavery movement from 1767 till his death in 1813.[104]

THE JAMES SOMERSET CASE

A white slave master, Charles Stewart left America in 1769 and came with his slave, James Somerset, to London. On arrival in London

James escaped from his master and found refuge in London's growing Black community.

He was eventually found, kidnapped and chained. He was sent to a ship on the River Thames ready to be sailed to Jamaica to work the plantations. His friends, with the help of Granville Sharp, issued a writ against the captain of the ship. The matter was referred to the Kings Bench for decision. In June 1772, Lord Mansfield agreed to free Somerset.

This caused euphoria in the Black communities up and down the country. Nearly 200 Blacks held a victory party in a public house in Westminster. Lord Mansfield, himself a slave owner ruled that while it was legal to own slaves it was illegal to take them from England by force.[105]

This caused shock waves amongst whites. The media whipped up the hysteria and demanded from Parliament that Blacks be expelled from Britain. Their main points of argument were ridiculous to say the least: -

Blacks had swamped all major cities and were responsible for all crimes committed.

Young pregnant white women, who had seen too many Black faces were terrified into giving birth to Black babies.

Blacks were enjoying lives of happiness and ease while their white counterparts were forced to starve and suffer on the streets.

London and other major cities would soon resemble Ethiopia.

THE BLACK LOYALISTS

In 1775, during the American War of Independence, the British offered freedom to American Black slaves who agreed to fight for the Crown - these Blacks were known as Loyalists.

When Britain lost the war these Loyalists came to England. Apart from their freedom they received no further reward for their services. They were reduced to begging on the streets. This once again renewed the race phobia and the call to expel all Black people from these shores was repeated.[106]

The number of Black beggars must have been staggering because they caught the attention of a group of merchants, MPs and bankers.

These concerned people formed themselves into an organisation called *Committee for the Relief of Black Poor*. They distributed daily relief and hospital care at Mile End and Lisson Green. The Committee soon decided that the best solution to the problem was separation. [107]

They adopted a plan devised by Henry Smeathman to resettle Blacks in Sierra Leone, West Africa. The Government backed the plan and helped sponsor the project. They employed eight Black men to try and persuade other Blacks to go back to Africa. They had little success.[108] They then took firmer action by refusing to give relief to those who would not sign to go back.

They also advertised that the public should refuse to aid Blacks that would not sign on the dotted line. When this also proved unsuccessful, they simply rounded up Blacks they found begging - whether they had signed or not - and forced them onto the waiting boats.

These Blacks were shipped to Africa's West Coast, a town called 'The Land of Freedom' today known as Free Town, the capital of Sierra Leone.[109]

The remaining Black population in Britain organised themselves into a formidable force to fight against these expulsions. According to newspaper reports of that time, East London's Whitechapel area was the assembly point for meetings. They did not trust the plan offered. They saw it as a wicked scheme to force them back into chattel slavery.

In 1803 Britain became involved in the Napoleonic wars. Britain needed Blacks to join the armed forces. Once again Blacks volunteered their services to fight for the Crown.

At the end of the war in 1815 (which Black people helped win for Britain), they returned to England with little thanks and reward. The result, once again, was the streets of London populated by Black beggars called 'vagrants'. However, a number of Blacks had worked themselves into the British society and became an intricate part of the system.[110]

THE BRITISH EMPIRE

Now that the British had waxed rich out of the African Atlantic slave trade, she had finance and power to invest in countries far outside her boundaries. She now controlled the seas after beating off the French and the Spanish - life had never been so good. Her worldwide empire was so vast that she boasted that the sun could never set on her.

All those that were in the Empire were considered British subjects regardless of race, colour or creed. Many of these Black 'subjects' were shipped to seaports like Cardiff, Liverpool, Glasgow and London. When the first and Second World War struck it was these 'subjects' that were called upon, along with overseas 'subjects', to once again fight to defend the British and her Empire.[111]

History was doomed to repeat itself once again, because these brave men and women received little or no thanks. In fact in 1919 race riots broke out in Liverpool, London, Cardiff and Newport.

White soldiers returning from war felt that the Blacks should not be taking their jobs and white women. Reports show that whole Black families had to attend police stations requesting protection. Newspaper reports of that time showed that the minority blacks did not sit back and take a beating; many of them fought back and defended themselves admirably.[112]

FROM WINDRUSH TO WINDS OF CHANGE- RESPECT DUE TO THAT FIRST GENERATION

During the Second World War each island in the Caribbean ran campaigns to draft men and women into the war. This proved very successful for the British Government. The Daily Mirror reported that over 10,000 Jamaicans alone volunteered and came to this country to fight. Eight thousand went into the armed forces and two thousand into munitions work.[113]

After the Second World War, Britain was in need of great help - the German blitzes had devastated parts of the country and the war had proven to be a great drain on her resources. The whole infrastructure had to be rebuilt; Britain turned to its trusted and faithful allies - the Blacks and Asians of her Empire.

On June 22, 1948 the ship SS Empire Windrush arrived at Tilbury Docks carrying 492 settlers from the Caribbean. These 492 settlers from the Caribbean arrived in Britain bringing with them a new way of life - things have not been the same ever since. Soon thousands more followed, they all carried British passports and were anxious about the prospects of their new life in Britain.

The SS Windrush was the first ship to bring over settlers to help fill the labour shortage just after the war. The British economy was short of workers and the government had been recruiting in the 'West Indies' for British Subjects to help rebuild the shattered post-war economy.

The arrival of the ex-troopship represents a pivotal point in modern British history. This first generation wasted no time.

Within three years Jamaicans alone had sent back over ten million pounds in postal orders to families overseas. The brothers in those days were not interested in having anything other than their own women. They soon sent for their wives and children.[114]

Many families would share one house, families sometimes confined to just one room. They worked tirelessly and soon were able to purchase decrepit houses in dilapidated condition and renovate it themselves. They took jobs in steel, coal, cotton, public transport and health care. They were law-abiding citizens from good families.

No islander was allowed to leave their island with a criminal record and three out of five of them belonged to a church. They were indeed model citizens. [115]

Conclusion

The more we introduce a balanced approach to British history is the more it will help improve understanding between the various racial groups.

When Black British history is researched and taught properly, the Black community may feel a sense of patriotism and help build a society based on freedom, justice and equality regardless of creed, class or colour.

The word patriot comes from the Latin word patriota, which means **father**. As pointed out and proved in earlier chapters, it was our ancestors that **fathered** the first civilisation in the United Kingdom.

The ignorance of this type of truth has made the majority of white people feel that they are better than everyone else.

They have created institutions that reflect this sense of superiority. It is this mindset of white supremacy that needs to die in order that the human family can live together in harmony.

There are two major problems that must be solved: White supremacy and Black inferiority. Both are equally destructive.

True history will help Europeans see they are not better just because their skin is paler than others. Leo Muhammad (Mr. Edutainment) teaches mixed audiences at Hyde Park, Speakers Corner in London, that white supremacy is a false pedestal that must be brought down because it is not based on truth.

Due to a lack of self-knowledge Black people - subconsciously - hate themselves and believe they are worse than all other people. The result is a destructive life style or what should be called death style.

This type of mind will breed lack of trust, non co-operation, disunity, Black-on-Black violence, drug taking... and the list goes on. A true, balanced reflection of history can help solve all of these problems - but any solution must begin with and involve our young.

When we look at the state education of Black youth- the literacy level, the drop out rate, test scores, truancy, plans for higher education and the cultivation of principles - the British school system has failed our youth. At present there is a quest to ascertain why Black children are drastically under achieving at school.

Black parents want to know why their children enter into the school system at the age of 5, bright eyed, studious and with an inquisitive mind, and yet 10 years later their desire to know and to acquire knowledge has been trampled and beaten to death.

The answer is stunningly simple: Black youths are not taught anything about SELF. A lack of the knowledge of 'self' – the soul - is the specific reason for the apathy of many of our children in schools. They are soul destroyed.

This gives a greater understanding of why the Ancient Egyptians (who as we now know were Black) - the master builders of temples and palaces all over the world - would carve over their temples and places of learning,

"MAN, KNOW THY-SELF".

A person's pursuit of knowledge be it formal or informal, should lead them to a better understanding of themselves and their environment.

If a photographer takes a picture of you in a crowd, then shows you that picture, by nature the first thing you would do is look for yourself. This is not vanity; we have a natural desire to know where we fit in the picture.

Today, education is only a tool to obtain a well-paid job for the sole purpose of acquiring money, cars and houses. It has been reduced to a means of attracting material wealth. However, we are making a fatal mistake.

We need to be reminded of what the purpose of true education is:

1 Education separates the human being from the beast in the field.

2 Education cultivates the person's mind spirit and soul.

3 Education satisfies our natural thirst to know.

4 Education is to teach us how to give correct service to self, family, community, nation and then to the world.

Proper education is vital to each individual's life chances and the quality of the society as a whole. If Britain does not wake up and recognise the consequences of continuing the current system of education, then the country's fate is sealed to doom.

References

1 World Book Encyclopaedia- Volume 12, Childcraft international, Inc page 141.

2 Afrikan People and European Holidays: A Mental Genocide Bk 2 - Rev Ishakamusa Barashango, IV Dynasty Publishing Company page 7.

3 World Book Encyclopaedia- Volume 6, Childcraft international Inc page 47.

4 World Book Encyclopaedia- Volume 13, Childcraft international Inc page 322b.

5 Sex and Race, Volume 1, J A Rogers, Helga M Rogers 1967, page 29.

6 Sex and Race, Volume 1, J A Rogers, Helga M Rogers 1967, page 29.

7 Exploding the Myths, Nile Valley Contributions to Civilisation, Anthony Browder,
   Institute of Karmic Guidance, page 52.

8 Wonderful Ethiopians of the Ancient Cushite Empire, Drusilla Dunjee Houston, Black Classic Press.

9 Herodotus, The Histories Book 2, Penguin Classics.

10 Exploding the Myths, Nile Valley Contributions to Civilisation, Anthony Browder,
    Institute of Karmic Guidance, page 103

11 Herodotus, The Histories Book 2, Penguin Classics, page 189

12 Herodotus, The Histories Book 2, Penguin Classics, page 189.

13 Wonderful Ethiopians of the Ancient Cushite Empire, Drusilla Dunjee Houston, Black Classic Press, page 211.

14 What they never told you in history class, Indus Khamit Kush, Luxorr Publications, page 190.

15 Sex and Race, Volume 1, J A Rogers, Helga M Rogers 1967, page 62.

16 Anacalypsis Volume 1, Godfrey Higgins, A&B Book Publishers, page 57.

17 Anacalypsis Volume 1, Godfrey Higgins, A&B Book Publishers, page 58.

18 The African Presence in Ancient America. They came before Columbus, Ivan Van Sertima, Random House, page 30.

19 Message to the Blackman in America, Hon Elijah Muhammad, Muhammad's Temple No2, page 108

20 Wonderful Ethiopians of the Ancient Cushite Empire, Drusilla Dunjee Houston, Black Classic Press, page 130.

21 The Holy Quran, Maulana Muhammad Ali, Speciality Promotions Co Inc, page1209.

22 Sex and Race, Volume 1, J A Rogers, Helga M Rogers 1967, page 67

23 Sex and Race, Volume 1, J A Rogers, Helga M Rogers 1967, page 68.

24 Sex and Race, Volume 1, J A Rogers, Helga M Rogers 1967, page 68.

25 Afrikan People and European Holidays: A Mental Genocide Bk 2 - Rev Ishakamusa Barashango, IV Dynasty Publishing Company page 7.

26 Sex and Race, Volume 1, J A Rogers, Helga M Rogers 1967, page 68.

27 The Theology of Time, The Honourable Elijah Muhammad, U.B & U.S Communications Systems, page 19.

28 What they never told you in history class, Indus Khamit Kush, Luxorr Publications, page 226.

29 What they never told you in history class, Indus Khamit Kush, Luxorr Publications, page 226.

30 Afrikan People and European Holidays: A Mental Genocide Bk 2 - Rev Ishakamusa Barashango, IV Dynasty Publishing Company, page 9.

31 Ancient Future, Wayne B Chandler, Black Classic Press, page 152.

32 World Book Encyclopaedia- Volume 17, Childcraft international Inc page 204.

33 Ancient Future, Wayne B Chandler, Black Classic Press, page 148.

34 Egypt Revisited, Ivan Van Sertima, Transaction Publishers, page 53.

35 World Book Encyclopaedia- Volume 17, Childcraft international Inc page 204.

36 Tynetta Muhammad, Mathematical Theology of Islam, Lecture.

37 Afrikan People and European Holidays: A Mental Genocide Bk 2 - Rev Ishakamusa Barashango, IV Dynasty Publishing Company, page 10.

38 Afrikan People and European Holidays: A Mental Genocide Bk 2 - Rev Ishakamusa Barashango, IV Dynasty Publishing Company, page 10.

39 Afrikan People and European Holidays: A Mental Genocide Bk 2 - Rev Ishakamusa Barashango, IV Dynasty Publishing Company, page 10.

40 Afrikan People and European Holidays: A Mental Genocide Bk 2 - Rev Ishakamusa Barashango, IV Dynasty Publishing Company, page 33.

41 World Book Encyclopaedia- Volume 1, Childcraft international Inc page 73.

42 World Book Encyclopaedia- Volume 1, Childcraft international Inc page 73.

43 World Book Encyclopaedia- Volume 1, Childcraft international Inc page 73.

44 Ancient and Modern Britons, David MacRitchie, France Preston, page 8.
45 Ancient and Modern Britons, David MacRitchie, France Preston, page 8.
46 Ancient and Modern Britons, David MacRitchie, France Preston, page 8.
47 Egypt Revisited, Ivan Van Sertima, Transaction Publishers, page 53.
48 Ancient and Modern Britons, David MacRitchie, France Preston, page 42.
49 Ancient and Modern Britons, David MacRitchie, France Preston, page 42.
50 Afrikan People and European Holidays: A Mental Genocide Bk 2 - Rev Ishakamusa Barashango, IV Dynasty Publishing Company, page 10.
51 Afrikan People and European Holidays: A Mental Genocide Bk 2 – Rev Ishakamusa Barashango, IV Dynasty Publishing Company, page 10
52 Afrikan People and European Holidays: A Mental Genocide Bk 2 - Rev Ishakamusa Barashango, IV Dynasty Publishing Company, page 10
53 Ancient and Modern Britons, David MacRitchie, France Preston, page 44.
54 Ancient and Modern Britons, David MacRitchie, France Preston, page 44.
55 Ancient and Modern Britons, David MacRitchie, France Preston, page 46.
56 Ancient and Modern Britons, David MacRitchie, France Preston, page 48.
57 Ancient and Modern Britons, David MacRitchie, France Preston, page 48.
58 Ancient and Modern Britons, David MacRitchie, France Preston, page 58.
59 Ancient and Modern Britons, David MacRitchie, France Preston, page 58.
60 Ancient and Modern Britons, David MacRitchie, France Preston, page 110.
61 Irish Names, Laurence Flanagan, Gill and Macmillian Ltd, page 58.
62 Ancient and Modern Britons, David MacRitchie, France Preston, page 134.
63 Ancient and Modern Britons, David MacRitchie, France Preston, page 113.
64 Ancient and Modern Britons, David MacRitchie, France Preston, page 113.
65 Ancient and Modern Britons, David MacRitchie, France Preston, page 54.
66 Ancient and Modern Britons, David MacRitchie, France Preston, page 53.
67 Ancient and Modern Britons, David MacRitchie, France Preston, page 137
68 Ancient and Modern Britons, David MacRitchie, France Preston, page 138.
69 Etymological Dictionary of the English Language, Rev Walter W Skeat, Oxford at the Clarendon Press.
70 Ancient and Modern Britons, David MacRitchie, France Preston, page 140.
71 Ancient and Modern Britons, David MacRitchie, France Preston, page 143.
72 Ancient and Modern Britons, David MacRitchie, France Preston, page 147.
73 Afrikan People and European Holidays: A Mental Genocide Bk 2 - Rev Ishakamusa Barashango, IV Dynasty Publishing Company, page 11.
74 World Book Encyclopaedia, Volume 18, Childcraft international, page 716
75 Afrikan People and European Holidays: Mental Genocide Bk 2 - Rev Ishakamusa Barashango, IV Dynasty Publishing Company, page 11.

76   Afrikan People and European Holidays: A Mental Genocide Bk 2 – Rev Ishakamusa Barashango, IV Dynasty Publishing Company, page 12.
77   Anacalypsis Volume 1, Godfrey Higgins, A&B Book Publishers, page 59.
78   Anacalypsis Volume 1, Godfrey Higgins, A&B Book Publishers, page 59.
79   Anacalypsis Volume 1, Godfrey Higgins, A&B Book Publishers, page 384.
80   Anacalypsis Volume 1, Godfrey Higgins, A&B Book Publishers, page 384.
81   Afrikan People and European Holidays: A Mental Genocide Bk 2 - Rev Ishakamusa Barashango, IV Dynasty Publishing Company, page 34
82   Afrikan People and European Holidays: A Mental Genocide Bk 2 - Rev Ishakamusa Barashango, IV Dynasty Publishing Company, page 38
83   Afrikan People and European Holidays: A Mental Genocide Bk 2 - Rev Ishakamusa Barashango, IV Dynasty Publishing Company, page 38.
84   Afrikan People and European Holidays: A Mental Genocide Bk 2 - Rev Ishakamusa Barashango, IV Dynasty Publishing Company, page 39
85   Afrikan People and European Holidays: A Mental Genocide Bk 2 - Rev Ishakamusa Barashango, IV Dynasty Publishing Company, page 41.
86   Afrikan People and European Holidays: A Mental Genocide Bk 2 - Rev Ishakamusa Barashango, IV Dynasty Publishing Company, page 39.
87   Hutchinson Pictorial Encyclopaedia, Walter Hutchinson.
88   Afrikan People and European Holidays: A Mental Genocide Bk 2 - Rev Ishakamusa Barashango, IV Dynasty Publishing Company, page 46
89   Prince Charles – Speech: Islam and the West – Oxford Centre for Islamic Studies, The Sheldonian Theatre, Oxford, 27/10/93.
90   Prince Charles – Speech: Islam and the West – Oxford Centre for Islamic Studies, The Sheldonian Theatre, Oxford, 27/10/93.
91   Prince Charles – Speech: Islam and the West – Oxford Centre for Islamic Studies, The Sheldonian Theatre, Oxford, 27/10/93.
92   World's Great men of colour, J A Rodgers, Helgar M Rodgers.
93   Sex and Race, Volume 1, J A Rogers, Helga M Rogers 1967, page 206.
94   World Book Encyclopaedia, Volume 13, Childcraft international, page 652.
95   Cadogan Guides, The Caribbean, James Henderson, Cadogan Books.
96   Cadogan Guides, The Caribbean, James Henderson, Cadogan Books.
97   Black Settlers in Britain 1555-1958, Nigel Files and Chris Power, Heinemann Educational Books Ltd.
98   Afrikan People and European Holidays: A Mental Genocide Bk 2 - Rev Ishakamusa Barashango, IV Dynasty Publishing Company, page 96.
99   The Black Holocaust for Beginners, S E Anderson, Writers and Readers Publishing Inc, page 36.

[100] The Black Holocaust for Beginners, S E Anderson, Writers and Readers Publishing Inc, page 34

[101] The Black Holocaust for Beginners, S E Anderson, Writers and Readers Publishing Inc, page 41

[102] Black Settlers in Britain 1555-1958, Nigel Files and Chris Power, Heinemann Educational Books Ltd, page 6.

[103] Black Settlers in Britain 1555-1958, Nigel Files and Chris Power, Heinemann Educational Books Ltd, page 15.

[104] Black Settlers in Britain 1555-1958, Nigel Files and Chris Power, Heinemann Educational Books Ltd, page 17.

[105] Black Settlers in Britain 1555-1958, Nigel Files and Chris Power, Heinemann Educational Books Ltd, page 14.

[106] Black Settlers in Britain 1555-1958, Nigel Files and Chris Power, Heinemann Educational Books Ltd, page 26.

[107] Black Settlers in Britain 1555-1958, Nigel Files and Chris Power, Heinemann Educational Books Ltd, page 28.

[108] Black Settlers in Britain 1555-1958, Nigel Files and Chris Power, Heinemann Educational Books Ltd, page 28.

[109] Black Settlers in Britain 1555-1958, Nigel Files and Chris Power, Heinemann Educational Books Ltd, page 34.

[110] Black Settlers in Britain 1555-1958, Nigel Files and Chris Power, Heinemann Educational Books Ltd, page 49.

[111] Black Settlers in Britain 1555-1958, Nigel Files and Chris Power, Heinemann Educational Books Ltd, page 46.

[112] Black Settlers in Britain 1555-1958, Nigel Files and Chris Power, Heinemann Educational Books Ltd, page 70.

[113] Daily Mirror, 9 September 1958.

[114] Daily Mirror, 9 September 1958

[115] Daily Mirror, 9 September 1958.